PRAISE FOR *SON OF THE CORNFIELD*

'Tragedy' is when something grossly unfair happens; 'triumph' is when something heroic overcomes. This book - this author - triumphs. Alexandru Lupu's memoir is intensely naked and vulnerable, as he invites the reader to truly know him. 'Son of the Cornfield' is a journey - across decades, countries, loves, and sexual identities - and the journey's end is still to be discovered.

—MIKE ROSEBUSH

From whatever walk of life you've come from, the extraordinary life revealed between these pages will find you at some of the most unprecedented cultural crossroads of our day. Enigmatic and effortlessly charming, Alexandru Lupu's story will keep you guessing, reassessing the narrative of our own soul, and perhaps find an unwavering purpose found in the fragility of life.

—JOHN CHEN

A boy is born in Romania and h
childhood, he experiences pain a
of a loving God, his life would h
village. Instead, Alex began a jou
more importantly, a slow and ste , ̣   ̣   ̣ ̣   ̣ ̣   ̣ . ̣ ̣ ̣ journey
took him far from his home, to the Netherlands, to Belgium and then across the world to Australia. He writes candidly about his encounters with men, from the rape of his childhood, to his search for love as he travels from one country to the next.

—SHIRLEY BASKETT

Upon receiving the manuscript unexpectedly, I read it in a single haul. Alex's autobiographical narration is so personal and painfully honest, that it rendered me, as a reader, uncomfortable. While aiming to find peace with himself, Alex disturbed my peace and has engraved his scars onto my heart permanently.

—JELLE CREEMERS

This book you hold in your hands is a treasure as rare as diamonds. Alex Lupu fearlessly shares his journey of growth through rejection, pain and abuse toward wholeness and Christlikeness. I pray his riveting story will move and challenge you as deeply as it did me.

—ROB EDWARDS

A wonderful portrait of God's love and redemption in the messiness of life. This memoir about finding one's self-identity and purpose. Alexandru Lupu writes with vulnerability which captivates the reader with marvellous storytelling.

—ROGER SANDRE

Beautiful prose and vivid dialogue from a vehicle on which the author takes us on a journey through his life up till now, vulnerable and open when he unfolds his inner world page by page.

A story of being torn between the desire to love and be loved by another man, and his faith in a different way of life through a plan that God has for him.

Between the lines is the narrative of a God who keeps His promise, who remains faithful when we are not, whose patience and grace covers us, and whose Spirit gently guides us where He wants us to be: into His loving arms.

And since authors develop throughout their career, this debut is a promise for more beauty to come. Certainly a must read.

—JAN DRAAIJER

Brutally honest - that is what this book by Alexandru Lupu is. It challenges, confronts and touches your heart. Son of the Cornfield makes you able to see that sexuality is something we really need to put on the Evangelical agenda. Its complexity is brought to the footlight with this challenging and honestly open read.

—ROCCO RAUSCH

SON
OF THE
CORNFIELD

A MEMOIR

...

ALEXANDRU LUPU

red flake
media

Red Flake Media
4 Pearl Gibbs Circuit
Canberra ACT 2914
Australia
Phone: (61 4) 5735 6856
Email: contact@alexandrulupu.com
Web: www.alexandrulupu.com

Editor: Jessica Perini
Cover Design: Erik Peterson
Text Layout: Erik Peterson
ISBN 9780646831091

For Alan

AUTHOR'S NOTE

For the last three years, I have been struggling with God. I felt that He was pushing me towards sharing my journey with other people, especially my friends and Christians from church. But I did not heed His call, because I was afraid that once they knew my entire story, they would no longer want to be my friends.

On a recent trip to Romania, everything changed. A young man in a Transylvanian village tried to kill himself because he felt that if his church knew about his same-sex attraction, he would be hated and expelled from their midst. I used to be like that man. His story impacted me so much that I decided to respond to God's gentle call in writing this book.

My goal is not to analyse homosexuality from a theological perspective, as dozens of books already do just that. I simply desire to share the story of how God has saved me from physical and spiritual death.

Son of the Cornfield is the account of a child who felt unloved and abused by his parents, raped by his 'friends', and harassed by attractions he could not understand, but who was embraced by his Creator and Saviour in ways he could not have possibly imagined.

I have altered most names, places, and certain details, in order to maintain the privacy of the people mentioned in this book.

ROOTS

LONELINESS

MY STORY BEGINS long before I drew my first breath.

It starts with Zoe, on her way home after a party after midnight, arm-in-arm with a girlfriend, five kilometres from her village. The old streetlamps created fleeting shadows of Zoe's tiny figure, high heels stumbling on the cobbled road.

"We need to find a rich boyfriend for you, Zoe! All that glamour is going to waste on a bunch of uneducated peasants," said her friend.

"Why complicate life? He'll want me to cook him dinner and wash his clothes and make babies! Where is the fun in that?" replied Zoe.

"But a nice car would make this journey so much more enjoyable, don't you think?"

"Maybe you're right. One day … we'll see," said Zoe.

As the two girls walked together, trading giggles and hearty laughs, a bear-like growl rose from up from the hills, startling them.

They increased their pace, glancing behind, panic rising with every step. As they walked through a valley, the growls echoed; where were they coming from?

Then they heard rumbling, and vibration shook the ground. A huge boulder tumbled out from the darkness, landing in front of Zoe. She froze. Her face drained, white as snow, her pupils dilated, and her breathing seemed to have stopped. She collapsed.

• • •

She regained consciousness back in her bed, the surge of the shock still vibrating in her body, like the smell of smoke after a fire. Every time she tried to close her eyes, she'd relive the powerlessness of that moment. The longest night of her life.

The next day she found out that it hadn't been a bear that made those sounds and had rolled the boulder down the hill, but a drunk man she used to go to school with. He thought that pranking the girls might be a good story to tell his mates the next day.

Zoe wasn't the same person after that night. Her mind was taken captive by an immense anxiety. The same fear of death that she experienced years ago when her mother, Flor almost killed her, now enveloped her with a force one thousand times stronger.

Later during the day, as the sun began to set, she started feeling distressed. The idea of darkness haunted her like a faceless demon. Every fibre of her being trembled. As the vibrations intensified, she felt a desire to run frantically around the garden. And so she did. She only realised she was barefoot after the sharp little rocks had cut into the soles of her feet leaving a bloody trail behind. That night she slept under the moonlight, curled up like a baby, unable to console herself.

A few days after the incident, Zoe decided to tell her parents what had happened.

"Why do you make such a fuss about this? I told you not to go out that night! Especially not dressed like that!" said Flor.

"What do my clothes have to do with the fact that I was pranked? Can't you see I am hurting?"

"The only thing I care about is that the animals haven't been fed while you are sulking. Stupid girl!" barked her mother.

"Don't talk to her like that! I will go out to the stables. Give me a minute," said Tiberius (Zoe's dad) gesticulating towards Flor to leave them on their own.

"Thank you, Father. She frightens me so much! Why can't she see I am in pain?" said Zoe letting thick tears soak into Tiberius's woollen jumper.

"Don't mind her, Zoe! She had a bad day. You're safe! Shhhh."

She felt her father's protective love and embraced him with all her strength. His callused hands caressed her back like a tuneless lullaby. When he gently pulled away, Zoe shifted her gaze to Tiberius' face for a moment. The love behind his brilliant blue eyes was all she needed to see.

As he left, Flor's words stalked her, "stupid girl, making such a fuss!"

• • •

Flor grew up in a Romanian hamlet at the edge of Buzau county, called Cărăbuşi (in Romania), the second of three children. Her older sister married very young, and her younger brother had left the family home, because he felt that farming was not his calling. So Flor at only thirteen years carried a tremendous responsibility to provide for her family; she felt the weight of the world on her shoulders.

The animals they'd bought two winters before were not even theirs; Flor's father had taken a loan from the mayor of the village, buying two bulls, three cows and a horse, hoping that his farm would be saved.

Flor would wake up every morning at first light, working the land, planting corn and vegetables on a small piece of land, a thirty-minute walk from the house. She'd come back after sunset – famished and too exhausted to do any homework. She loved reading about princesses and their magical castles. Seeing their two-bedroom house always broke Flor's spell; instead of a castle she lived under a curse.

Her family's poverty felt like an unbreakable chain. She could not go to high school like the other girls from the village. The only way to escape the misery she'd lived in all her life was marriage.

● ● ●

Flor was nineteen when she met Tiberius at a village fair. She fancied his stature and his brilliant blue eyes.

"I haven't seen you here before, miss! Are you from the Valley?" said the young man.

"Yes, I grew up here. And yes, this is the first time I've been to the fair. But I don't know how to dance, so I don't see why I should make a fool of myself," retorted Flor.

"Come! Let me show you. Just follow my lead!

Abandoning herself in Tiberius' arms, Flor muted the voices in her mind pestering her with the problems she'd left at home. No more images of her sick father and her dominant mother; she just took pleasure in being seen, touched, appreciated.

Tiberius looked deep into her eyes that first evening. Flor knew that she had finally found her man. No longer did she need to be a slave. For the first time she felt free, like the goose they used for filling up bed cushions.

Seven months later, they got married. They wanted an intimate wedding, with only their parents, siblings, and a handful of close friends. After the civil officiation and the church service, which took only two hours, they headed back to the house, celebrating until after sunset.

Tiberius had inherited his house after both his parents died during a pneumonia outbreak. At just seventeen and an orphan, with a young sister in his care, he took a job in carpentry in Nehoiu, a small mountain town thirty kilometres from their village.

He loved the tranquillity of his life, and the multiple journeys per day from the house to their patch of arable land, just to see Flor. She would often bring her picnic basket and have lunch with her handsome husband. Tiberius' dark hair reminded her of the colour of the horse she rode growing up.

Three years after their wedding, Flor fell pregnant. On that same August of 1965, Romania became a Socialist Republic. No one knew what the future might bring. Engrossed in the speech blasted from the radio, Tiberius looked worried for a second when Flor gave him the news about the baby, but he dismissed his pessimism with a hearty smile.

"We're going to be parents, Flor! Imagine that!"

"I'd love to have a boy! He will be so handsome!" said his wife.

"May God keep him safe, dear; the rest will be fine."

On her way back, Flor's mind drifted. She couldn't be happy. Months ago, she had given herself to another man at the village fair. She'd drunk too much, the alcohol loosening her inhibitions. As the shepherd made love to her, the bucolic smell of sheep and whey imbued in his skin soothed her. She buried the memory so deep she wouldn't be tempted to remember. *I promise I won't cheat on Tiberius anymore. He will never know.*

. . .

Flor had never shown affection to her daughter. On a sunny May morning, as Zoe came back from the store with the ingredients for her tenth birthday cake, Flor refused to help her bake it.

"Why are you so cruel to me?" wailed the child.

"You simply don't deserve it!"

"But why? What have I done to you to punish me so harshly?"

"You weren't conceived in love! You were just the fruit of a fling. An accident," said Flor staring out the window.

Zoe stood motionless behind her mother, unable to comprehend what she'd just heard. *Is my father not my real father? I thought he loved Mum! How can I be an accident? My own mother hates me. Are Claudiu and Christian my brothers?*

Zoe knew not to press with more questions. As she kneaded the dough, tears fell into the mixture.

Claudiu came into the kitchen, after playing football with his mates in their back garden.

"Happy birthday, sis! May you grow big and fat like that dough you've just made!"

"Claudiu, don't say that! Thank you! Give me a kiss, you cheeky bugger!"

Her little brother always had a way of making her happy. He was so energetic and gave her the best kisses.

Flor loved Claudiu from the moment the nurse put him in her arms on that November morning in 1973. She saw Tiberius' eyes and nose in her newborn son. The guilt she had been carrying all those years vanished like a cloud. Claudiu was her husband's legitimate child.

"We have a baby boy, Flor! I cannot believe that!" shouted Tiberius.

"I am so happy, dear! I know how much you wanted a son!"

"Zoe will be so happy to meet her little brother!" said Tiberius.

"No ... not yet. Let me enjoy my baby a bit more!"

• • •

When Claudiu would damage the tools in his father's shed, Zoe took on the blame. She hated seeing him cry when he'd be punished. Even if Flor saw the girl's little acts of sacrifice, she never acknowledged that to her daughter.

When Flor was pregnant again Zoe prayed, *Please God, don't let my mother's venom be transferred to the new baby.* Once Tiberius and Flor's second boy, Christian, was born Flor's patience seemed lit on an even shorter fuse, as she'd beat Christian every time he was naughty. Seeing her brother hit on his lower back made Zoe fear for him, but she was too afraid to confront Flor. Zoe would take Christian in her arms and calm him down by caressing his handsome face.

• • •

Tiberius would wake at five every morning, to take the train to a town thirty kilometres away where he worked as a carpenter. He'd come home in the evening around eight. Only on Saturdays and Sundays could Zoe spend time with him – while working together on their small farm with their cows, poultry and sheep. He was a gentle spirit and he enjoyed listening to her silly stories from school.

"You will always be your father's daughter! You know that, right?"

"Yes Father. I love you the most of everyone in this world!" said Zoe.

"Don't let your mother steal your wonderful joy, my dear! She is trying her best. She sees life differently than us. She'll come around. Now, let me hear another one of your stories," said Tiberius with a child-like voice.

• • •

Tiberius loved his train trip to work. Most mornings he'd spend the journey asleep. Otherwise he'd just look outside the window and admire the landscape. His dream was to buy land and build a small farm where he could have more cows, more sheep, and maybe a couple of horses.

But once the kids were born, his dream became impossible. Zoe was already in Year 5 and her studies required money they didn't have. Selling a cow to pay for her education wasn't a big sacrifice. For him, at least. But Flor always resented spending the money on Zoe.

Tiberius could not understand Flor's animosity towards his daughter. She was so sweet to him, making him smile with her jokes she'd learn from school. Wanting to make her happy, he'd take a day off work and take her to a fair in a neighbouring village. He put on his Sunday clothes and asked her to put on a beautiful dress.

"You look like a princess, Zoe!"

"I am your princess, Father! Now, let's find me a prince!" said Zoe giving Tiberius a kiss on the cheek.

• • •

For Zoe being at the fair brought back memories of a big secret she carried. When she was only nine years old, she had come home early from school to get ready for a fair in their village. She could not wait to put on her silly folk costume and play with her girlfriends.

As she reached the house, she found the gate was locked. After she jumped the fence, she could hear giggles and laughter from inside the house. When she opened the door, her mother was in bed with a man she did not recognise. Her mother saw her and became furious, screaming at her.

"What are you doing home so early?" Get out, you stupid girl!" screamed Flor covering her naked breasts with the sheets.

Zoe closed the door behind her, ran outside, and began crying.

Flor came out and slapped her daughter throwing her on the ground.

"That should teach you not to meddle in things you are not supposed to!" yelled Flor.

Zoe hit her head on a rock and lay motionless for minutes. When she regained consciousness, she ran towards the barn where the hay was stored for the winter, tears streaming.

"I hope you stay hidden there for the rest of your life. If you ever tell anybody, I will kill you! You stupid girl!" screamed Flor.

After this incident, Zoe's relationship with her mother grew even colder. Terrified, she decided not to tell her father what had happened.

• • •

Now, almost a decade after catching her mother with the mysterious man, she finally realised what she'd witnessed. The contempt she felt for Flor grew stronger every day. She could have died that day, but what infuriated her the most was the betrayal of her father. *Was that the only time?* she wondered.

She remembered a morning when she was playing with her doll in the barn; she heard her mother yelling at someone. Peering through a hole in the wall, she recognised the voice of a family friend, shouting "How many more children will you throw in the river?" Not understanding what the woman meant, Zoe went back to playing.

But now, as a grown-up woman, she knew that the neighbour was referring to her mother's aborted children. She couldn't stand the thought of Flor cheating on Tiberius repeatedly. How many brothers and sisters could she have had if Flor had not terminated those pregnancies?

Telling her father about Flor's sexual adventures would only make things worse. If he found out about his wife's secret life that would have killed the wonderful light inside him.

Zoe's panic attacks grew in intensity and frequency; she needed her father now more than ever. But the phantoms of the past were the least of her concerns. The future terrified her now.

• • •

The couple of months following the prank boulder attack passed very slowly. Zoe's girlfriends stopped checking in on her, so she felt even more alone. One morning, on the way to the village store she met Tim, a gypsy-style middle-aged neighbour working on a drilling rig in the Carpathian Mountains. (The Communist regime planned as many drilling rigs as possible in the southern part of Romania, so many men from the region found employment thanks to the new scheme.)

"Zoe, I know a guy you should meet!" he said. "An electrician who works with me on the rig. A good-looking man with a great sense of humour."

"Thanks Tim, but I'm not up to meeting men at the moment. I have a lot of things on my plate."

"Well, you have to meet someone, soon! Your mother wants you married!"

"Who told you that?" asked Zoe.

"Well, the women in the village are like a telegraph."

"I am only twenty-three, Tim. There is still enough time," said Zoe.

"He will come visit me this weekend. Just talk to him. If you don't like him, no harm done. He has a motorcycle, you'll like that," Tim added.

"We'll see! Good to see you, Tim!"

Zoe didn't have the courage or strength to think about her future family. The final exams for school, ever demanding work on the farm, and the panic attacks kept her busier than she'd wanted. How could she envision a life away from her mother, devoid of fear and pain, when the present was as bitter as the fodder she fed the pigs with?

• • •

Saturday came sooner than she expected. It was a beautiful summer evening, so she'd bought a flowery strapless dress that'd go well with her yellow high-heeled shoes. It had been so long since she'd used make-up and done anything special with her hair. The mirror showed a good-looking young woman, with jet black hair, green eyes and a mysteriously faded smile.

Tim lived a couple of kilometres to the north, in a wooden cabin by the river. As she approached the house, she could hear music coming from inside and the sound of men laughing. Tim looked elated to see her.

With his usual grin, he called out: "Oh, hey! You came … Come and say hello to Radu!"

"Nice to meet you, Radu. I am Zoe."

"Pleased to finally meet you, Zoe. I've heard great things about you," said Radu.

"Oh, have you? I wonder who from?" teased Zoe, eying Tim.

Radu admired her dress, analysing her from head to toe.

"Beautiful motorbike, Radu. I like the green stripes!" said Zoe.

"I'd love to give you a ride soon," he replied.

"I've never been on one, but I might take you up on that … once I muster enough courage," Zoe added shyly.

● ● ●

That evening Zoe forgot about her problems. Radu was witty and treated her like a woman. She admired his shoulder-length raisin black hair and liquorice black eyes; his pupils immersed in the blackness of his irises.

Would I feel safe in his arms? She wondered. *Could he protect me from the world, from the indifference of my mother? How can I tell him that I am afraid of my own future? Do I even have one?*

At midnight she decided to leave; her jaw muscles aching from laughter.

"You are a delightful woman, Zoe. I am looking forward to seeing you again."

"Maybe I'll take you up on that offer," she said, pointing towards the motorbike.

When she got home everyone was already in bed. She knew she'd not sleep, but she didn't care. She could think of the future now. She might've found her saviour.

UNGOVERNED

ELENA HAD JUST TURNED TWENTY when she had her first child with George. She decided to call him Radu. She said to herself, "I had to give birth to my first child on my own, with no one's help, and God gave me victory." It wasn't customary for Romanian men to be present with their wives when they were in labour, so George was asked to wait outside the room.

He did not mind, he was hypnotised by the radio – Sputnik 2 had reached the Earth's orbit, with Laika (the dog) on board. He had followed the developments ever since Sputnik 1 had been launched in October that year. He could speak a bit of Russian, so he followed the dialogue between the Russian scientists with ease.

He was so absorbed in the excitement of the space exploration, that he did not hear Elena's shrieks coming from the other room. After a couple of hours, the midwife placed his newborn son in his arms.

"He is gorgeous, isn't he?" said the midwife.

"May he become an explorer ... like Laika!" suggested George.

George could not recognise any of his features in his newborn, but he dismissed any doubt that he might not be his father. He did not want to believe the rumours circulating in the village about Elena.

. . .

Radu was very quiet, happy being left on his own. Elena loved that about her baby, as she wouldn't be at home very often. She had a passion for adventure and living her life exuberantly. She knew every woman living in the village and most likely all the men, too. All gossip would first go through her, like a museum curator. She decided what gossip was worthy of propagating and what wasn't worth the effort.

As George was a passive man, she looked beyond him for love and adventure. She craved the attention of men. Inside her, she carried an insatiable desire to dominate every man she met.

One autumn morning, on her way to the village shops Elena saw a guy she'd never seen before, a tall muscular man, with a commanding presence, sitting on his parents' porch, smoking.

As she walked by, he laid eyes on her and his breath was taken away.

He worked as a colonel in the Romanian army, and he'd only come home to visit his parents once every couple of years.

"I've never seen you before in the village!" said Elena.

"I wanted to see my parents for Christmas before going back to the garrison. Are you a local?" asked the man.

"Yes. I was born in Cislău. Such a boring village, isn't it? I am sure you have seen a lot of the world."

"Do you have time for a drive? I know a nice restaurant in Buzău. We could have lunch there. I promise I will bring you back by sunset."

"Such a wonderful idea!" answered Elena.

An hour later, she found herself in the back seat of a Dacia 1100, giggling and absorbing this young man's attentions. On their way back to the village, she asked him to drop her off near the Purple Forest. She loved to smell the flowers at the edge of the forest and to talk to them. Little did she know that she was two weeks' pregnant at the time.

• • •

She could not forget her little romance with the colonel. She could see parts of him in Radu, and it drove her mad. His caresses were still etched into her skin like invisible tattoos. She'd have liked to be pursued by George her husband, desired even. She'd have loved him to make her feel like a woman, just like the colonel did, but she waited in vain. As the years passed, they'd drift apart even more.

When Elena gave birth to their second child, she wished that George would be more involved in his children's lives. But she realised that her hope would embitter her even more. Her newborn daughter was the female version of George; quiet and softly spoken. *Do I have enough love inside me to be a good mother to her? Every time I look at you, dear baby, I am reminded of how lonely I am. God, help me love her!*

• • •

George was a bike repairer and an apiarist. His patience was so inexhaustible that he could spend days abrading bicycle spokes, giving them back their original lustre. Only one metre-seventy tall, his appearance didn't inspire awe or admiration, he'd fade into the background in the presence of other men. All his life he had to brush off comments about his snubby nose.

Bees were his life. No one was allowed to join him when he was collecting the honey from the honeycombs. Radu always wanted to be initiated into this mysterious ritual, but he never got that privilege. From a very young age, he became jealous of the bees for absorbing so much of his father's attention.

In his own way, George loved Radu and his little sister, but he didn't know how to show it. The more Radu grew up, the more he began doubting whether he was his father. His height, the way he was built, and his energetic personality, was nothing like him. But he had no intention of confronting Elena. After all, George had raised Radu as his son.

George's love for Elena was rational, never driven by lust and power. His sexual drive was like a sparkplug that had lost its ability to form electricity. His parents arranged the wedding with Elena's family, without the young couple's input. Elena came from a very good family, with land and property – the perfect dowry in 1950s Romania.

The house built by George's grandfather was small. Perched on a hill, the view was breathtaking. As the summer evening air cooled, he loved going up to the attic watching the river as it travelled through the valley in front of the Ursoaia hills. As a child, he spent countless mornings fishing in the river.

From an early age he realised he could connect better with nature than with people. His inability to form human connections eventually drove his wife to find solace in someone else's arms. When Radu was seven and his sister four, Elena packed her bags and left him for another man.

"Radu, do you want to come with your sister and I?" asked Elena.

"Why do I have to choose between you and my grandparents?"

"… and you father!" added Elena.

"No. I will stay because my Grandma is ill. How can I leave her alone?"

"You can come back every other week. I am sure she'll understand," said his mother.

"No, she won't. She said you are a tramp. I want to stay with them!"

"Well, you can always change your mind! Goodbye son," said Elena kissing Radu on the cheek.

He never asked his father about Elena anymore. He missed his sister, but he could not see his mother; not after she'd left him. His Grandma died after a couple of years, and with her, any desire to be reunited with Elena.

·　·　·

George became even more distant after his wife moved away. The house that once was full of laughter, clamour and wilting flowers, was now empty, sad and lifeless. Secretly, he hoped that his wife would come back eventually, but she never did.

Nine years after Elena left, George met another woman, a hard-working divorcee from a village eighty kilometres away. She came to Cislău because of the cooperative established by the Communist party, where she started working at the stables.

George liked the stillness about her, and he hoped Radu, now fourteen, would have a mother again. But his son never accepted his father's new wife; he was already independent and didn't think he needed to be taken care of anymore.

"Why do you talk so harshly to her, son?" asked George.

"She is not my mother! Mother abandoned me. Why would I want to go through that again?"

"She won't do that, son. She is not like your mother."

"How do you know?" asked Radu with teary eyes.

"She is doing her best ... I know she does," responded George, trying to comfort his son.

. . .

A year after they got married, George's new wife gave birth to a boy. He became the centre of attention for George. For the first time, he adored being a father. A sparkle in George's core kindled as he held his newborn son for the first time. This time he didn't have to doubt whether he was the father, because the baby had his eyes, his cheeks and his elusive smile.

Radu loved his half-brother. He took him on walks in the forest and told him stories about electronic robots conquering the world. The love he felt for his baby brother surprised him and made him forget about his mother, whom he missed from time to time.

. . .

Radu concentrated on his studies even more after the arrival of his half-brother. He reasoned that if he could excel, he might get a scholarship and escape his life. He felt like an appendix to his family, someone who had no function and could easily be removed.

Radu soon realised that his dreams of continuing his studies would shatter into a million pieces. When he finished high school, his father fell ill, and he was obliged to work, so he could pay the bills and provide for his family.

He loved working as an electrician. Having to ride his motorbike for more than forty kilometres each way meant that he could freely explore his thoughts. Inventions with circuit boards and electricity filled his mind on the long journey.

● ● ●

A couple of years later, he'd find another job at a drilling mine as part of a team of electricians. There he befriended Tim, a short bloke with olive skin and with a funny Romanian accent. For the first time in his life, Radu felt that he finally belonged. Tim was from the same county and not that far from the village where Radu's parents lived. Together, the new friends spent countless weekends drinking and telling endless stories till deep in the night. Occasionally, they went motorbike riding together.

One evening, Radu's life would change forever. He was at Tim's place, in the garden, smoking a cigarette when a beautiful young woman in a flowery dress smiled at him. He froze for a moment uttering a skittish "hey!" They hit it off right away, and for the next few months they'd see each other every weekend.

COALESCENCE

WITH THE COUNTRY IN TURMOIL, after the execution of President Nicolae Ceauşescu a few months before, Radu feared losing his job, jeopardising any hope of a wedding day. But to his great surprise – the drilling rigs continued to pump out petroleum. His employment was secure.

The wedding day came sooner than Zoe expected. She was well aware of what a traditional Romanian wedding looked like: almost the whole village would be invited, live folk music, lots of *ţuică* (distilled plums) and dancing the whole night long.

Flor, Tiberius, and Claudiu – Zoe's brother – came to Cislău two days before the wedding. Flor helped Zoe clean the house and decorate every room with branches of fir tree (an evergreen, symbolising the longevity of the marriage). Tiberius and Radu were in charge of ensuring they had enough *ţuică*, wine and other drinks for the celebration. Claudiu was delighted for his sister. It was also his first wedding where he could drink and was rather excited about whom he might meet.

"I'll miss having you in the house, sis!" said Claudiu, with his usual smirk.

"And I will miss our talks. Good luck with Mother! You will be on your own!"

"Well, you know she loves *me*!" gushed Claudiu.

"Don't rub that in on my special day! You know, I wish she was happy for me. I have so much to learn about how to be a wife. I'll never ask *her* that," said Zoe, fighting back tears.

"Enough of that! It is the happiest day in your life. Radu seems like a great guy. He'll love you, I'll make sure of that."

"Thank you, my dear brother. Now, let me get changed ... there are so many things left to do," said Zoe, giving Claudiu an affectionate kiss on the cheek.

● ● ●

Tiberius was overwhelmed with fear. His daughter whom he loved more than anybody in the world was getting married to a man he barely knew. He only knew one thing about Radu: he grew up in a broken home.

Tiberius wanted to have a serious conversation with his future son-in-law about what happened to Zoe recently, but his wife convinced him not to. "Let her find her own happiness," said Flor, "He'll make *your* daughter happy." As he sat on the bench outside, looking at the stars, he was still wondering whether he had made a mistake not telling Radu about Zoe's panic attacks. After having seen half-a-dozen doctors and also a couple of witches, no one knew what was going on. What if Radu left her once he discovered the person she really was? Icy shivers flooded his body.

● ● ●

Flor loved feeling needed. The front door of Zoe's future home led to the kitchen, a three-by-three square room adorned with handmade woven carpets on the wall and on the floor. On the left side of the room, as you entered, was a custom-made fireplace on which Flor was cooking hundreds of *sarmale*, a traditional Romanian dish (a mixture of meat, rice, spices, rolled in sour cabbage leaves). The room was sparsely furnished but adorned with colourful carpets. Like a never sleeping vigilant, a large Orthodox icon featuring saint George dominated the eastern wall.

Next to the kitchen was a bedroom, also used as a living room. Just a tiny bit bigger than the kitchen, it contained a bed, a tv table on which sat a black-and-white Electronica tv set (a wedding gift given to them by their godparents).

A couple of days before the wedding, Flor had painted the walls in teal with vertical aubergine flowery motifs along the corners.

From the western wall a couple of stairs led to Radu's bedroom. A bit bigger than the previous two rooms, soon to be the master bedroom, this room was flooded in natural light. The floor was covered with a salmon pink Persian rug beautifully decorated with abstract Middle Eastern patterns. Next to the chiffonier, a door led to the last and largest room of the house, then used as a storage space. Radu's idea was to use a part of the money received at the wedding to decorate and furnish it, in order to use it as a guest bedroom.

He had big plans for the house. Dreaming of an extension, he wanted a bedroom for each child – he yearned for three boys. He'd never abandon them as Elena, his mother, did to him.

. . .

Zoe loved the garden, with its six walnut trees spread across the eight thousand square metres. At the back of the garden two plum orchards were divided by a long strip of arable land. She could already imagine the cornfield and vegetable patches on which she'd love to work in summer. Zoe had absorbed everything Flor taught her about horticulture (probably the only thing she appreciated about her mother).

Tiberius instilled in his daughter a love for the land. She was the only one who joined him voluntarily on his journeys to the grassland they'd bought when Zoe graduated. During mowing season, at the beginning of June, she would help Tiberius make haystacks. She had been so full of energy. But it all seemed to disappear in that dreadful night of the boulder. Could she ever be the same again? No one knew.

. . .

Radu's hobby repairing electronic devices – radios and tv sets – made him popular among the townspeople. Hundreds came to his wedding, festively dressed and excited about the party, which would last for twenty-four hours.

Radu would have to stop his adventures now. Up until this wonderful day, he loved to travel everywhere on his precious Mobra (a popular motorcycle brand from the Communist era made in Brașov). Numerous summer romances and memories drew him to Constanța like a beacon. But no more. Today he'd have to pledge his faithfulness to only one woman: Zoe.

He hoped that his marriage would restore his faith in women. None of his fleeting relationships did that. Something about Zoe told him that she was special. Her calm and her endearing personality made him feel safe. *Please God, don't allow her to abandon me too. Make our love last. Heal my broken heart through Zoe's loyalty and tenderness.*

• • •

She looked like an angel in her wedding dress given to her by her godmother's daughter. Because Zoe was twenty centimetres shorter, the dress had needed shortening. Always a reason to dislike herself, her height was both a blessing and a curse – made her feel insecure about herself, but also pushed her to try out the most extravagant stilettos.

With the veil on her head, her eyes were the first thing one would notice about her face; one was light brown and the other dark green. The dress sculpted her face in a white lace frame accentuating the difference.

Checking herself in the mirror, she couldn't believe how her face radiated. Her bridesmaids, Radu's cousin and his half-sister, helped Zoe with her make-up, hairstyle and dress. She was ready.

Radu waited for her in the kitchen, more handsome than ever, wearing an ivory suit with a maroon tie, his ebony hair swept back, and his black olive eyes smiling. His groomsman Emil, anxiously awaited Zoe's descent down the stairs.

As she came through the door, everyone clapped, and the musicians played a cheerful tune on the accordion as the guests drew near to see the bride in her dress. As he took her hands in his, Radu kissed her coral lips.

"You look wonderful, my dear," whispered Radu in his fiancé's ear.

"And you're so handsome. I love you, dear! I can't wait to be your wife," whispered Zoe.

Tiberius, who stood in a corner of the room, let a tear escape his weary eyes. He knew he had to show happiness, but something inside held him back. Flor gave Zoe a hasty peck on the cheek as she clapped along. "You better hide that side of you really well today," whispered Flor. Zoe lost her smile for a moment, but she wouldn't let her mother's malice ruin her day.

• • •

The Orthodox church was only twenty minutes away, so, they went on foot, together with the guests, accompanied by folk accordion, applause, drinking, shouting and laughing. Neighbours would come out of their houses and shout "*Casă de piatră*" [may your relationship be as strong and powerful as a stone house], at that time the strongest type of building material.

They finally reached the church perched atop a hill. Zoe glanced up at its towering presence with a sense of reverence and awe; this was her first time in this church. As they crossed the narthex of the church, the bell rang, and the bride and bridegroom approached the altar.

The smell of incense made Zoe feel sick and dizzy. She distracted herself by admiring the icons and Biblical scenes on the walls and ceiling. The eyes of the saints seemed to follow her every move.

Radu felt uncomfortable when Tiberius gave him Zoe's hand at the altar without looking into his eyes. The sting of disapproval coming from his future father-in-law, awoke a troubling realisation. *He didn't have the guts to tell me he doesn't like me. No wonder Flor takes all the decisions in that house. Tiberius is so weak, just like my father. I'd never let a woman control me. Not*

38

even Zoe. This epiphany kindled a war between Radu and Zoe's father; a battle that would consume Radu all his life.

The ceremony lasted a little over an hour and afterwards they were both hungry. The sponge fingers of the Eucharist celebration only made them even more ravenous.

Outside the church they were offered more *ţuică*. Some of the guests – especially the bachelors invited by Radu – were visibly tipsy. Cars waited on the main street to bring them to Ciuta Inn, where the party would take place.

● ● ●

Everyone danced that night; the musicians didn't stop. This was everything Zoe imagined as a child. Every guest was happy. Every man wanted to dance with her. But inside, a small shiver grew, like a storm cloud on a summer day. Her dazzling smile faded, no matter how much she tried to feign it.

She thought the early autumn air outside would help. With no one around, she started crying as if she could foresee her future life unravelling. The cold, the feeling of loneliness, and the pangs of fear clasped her in an ominous embrace, darker than the boulder of all those years ago.

Back inside the inn, once she finally took a seat, Zoe instinctively put her hand on her belly, rhythmically caressing it. *Is it possible I am already pregnant?* Few weeks ago, she made love to Radu the night after they had the civil officiation at the townhall. She hoped becoming a mother would drive those fears away. She had every right to be happy.

CONSANGUINEOUS

ZOE LOVED BEING PREGNANT, and she adored April mornings. As she woke, her room was inundated with light. Rapt in the smell of plum trees in bloom, she walked barefoot on the emerald green grass drenched in morning dew.

Radu's shift work meant he could be at home for two weeks, taking care of his wife but then, the next two weeks had to be away. Those days were tough for Zoe as she disliked being on her own and she found it hard to make friends with the women from the village. Flor lived thirty kilometres away, too difficult to visit her daughter regularly. But Zoe didn't mind.

Being a mum herself, memories about her childhood came back like an unwanted guest. The death of Christian had occupied her mind over the last few weeks. Even though it happened eight years ago, when she was seventeen and Claudiu five, it still felt raw.

Christian had been bathing in the river when he stopped breathing. One of his friends came running into the house saying that her brother had lost consciousness. Zoe was listening to U2's new album *War*, when she heard the news.

Tiberius fell into a trance. Flor, together with Christian's godmother, had brought her son inside warming up his body with blankets. Moments later, with his son's body laid out before him, Tiberius ran to his neighbour to ask whether he could drive them to the hospital.

The doctors couldn't do anything for his son. Christian had experienced kidney failure.

As Tiberius held his son's dead body on the way home, cold tears soaked his cheeks. What might've caused this? Flor would hit the boy's lower back when he was naughty, but surely that couldn't have led to her son's death. Or could it?

* * *

As her husband brought his dead son into the house, Flor yelled and cried over Christian's body. Zoe could not deal with the pain anymore. She ran until she reached the next village, seven kilometres away. *What if I told my father how Mum beat Christian? Maybe he would have stopped her from punishing him so mercilessly! What if I could have saved him? He would still be alive now! What have I done?*

She couldn't believe it. Playing with Christian gave her so much joy and helped her forget her own torment. She could still feel the bite mark left by Christian on her arm from the day before. She wished she could etch that forever into her skin.

Now it was too late to tell her father. Her precious little brother was gone. No one had noticed she had been away. Tiberius was inconsolable while Flor still wailed from Christian's room. *Stop pretending, you cold-blooded creature*, thought Zoe hearing her mother's cries. *You never loved him.*

* * *

As the memories came flooding into her mind, she suddenly felt cramps in her abdomen. Radu was at work, not expected back until five days later. The pain would not subside, so she called the ambulance.

The journey to the hospital felt like an eternity. The paramedics gave her something to calm her down, but the pills didn't seem to have any effect. The smell of the hospital made her even sicker. While she was waiting for the doctor to call her in, she went to the toilets, and stopped in shock when she saw the fear of losing her baby branded on her face in the mirror. She tried to wipe her tears away with her shaking hands as the nurse came in looking for her.

The doctor told her that her appendix was infected, and that she'd need to be operated on. What she heard next felt like the world crushing in on her. "In order to perform the operation, we need to abort the baby while your own life will be at risk as well," said the doctor in a grave voice. She fled the building in her hospital gown, barefoot, and wept like never before.

As she held her pregnant belly, she felt a kick. She collapsed into a foetal position, caressing her belly, screaming "My baby, my baby."

Two nurses came looking for her and they helped her back into the hospital. The doctors wanted to admit her as soon as possible. But she refused the abortion and the removal of her appendix. The emergency doctors pressured and pressured.

Four hours later, Radu came, still dressed in his work clothes, smelling of Vaseline and rusty iron. After he talked to the doctor that took on Zoe's case, he made a phonecall and asked the nurses to prepare the release paperwork for his wife.

"I won't let you do that to my wife and child!" barked Radu, helping Zoe to put her clothes back on, as another doctor came into Zoe's room.

"She is going to die, sir! As is her child," warned the doctor. "She needs to have the operations."

"We're leaving! I found another solution," blurted Radu.

On the way home, Radu explained to Zoe that a doctor in Cislău who had a private practice specialising in plant-based medicine might be able to help them. When they arrived in the village the doctor gave Zoe a pill the size of a two-dollar coin that was meant to temporarily attack the appendix infection which would buy her a few months for her child to come full term.

After she took the pill, the pain slowly subsided. Radu stayed at home with her for the next few weeks, in case her health deteriorated.

A few months later, at two in the morning, Zoe's waters broke. Radu phoned the village priest with whom he was good friends, and the priest drove them to the hospital in Nehoiu. Five and a half hours later, little Alexandru Gabriel was born.

◦ ◦ ◦

I was welcomed into this world on a sunny summer morning, Monday, 3 June 1991, and stayed with Mum in the hospital for the next five days. The maternity ward came alive, as I was passed around to every nurse and visitor, each commenting on how handsome they thought I was. My mum and dad glowed with pride. My grandmother couldn't stop herself from staring at me and holding me. For the first time, my mum felt that Flor respected her; she was a woman and she had given birth to a beautiful child.

My uncle, Claudiu, could not stop grinning. He would put me back in my cot only when he could not bear the ache in his arms.

"If I'm ever to be a father, I want a child just like him! He is so handsome, sis!"

"We have a good gene pool, *fratello* (my mother's recent appellation for her brother, inspired by the Italian films she was watching)!"

"I'll take you mowing with me soon, little man. You'll love the smell of cut grass," whispered Claudiu as he gave me a peck on the cheek.

• • •

Mum loved *Alexandru*, which in Greek means protector of men. Little did she know that this name would have a prophetic significance in my life. She chose my middle name, *Gabriel*, because my godmother's daughter was called Gabriela and my parents were expected to name me after her. As with my first name, the Hebrew origin of *Gabriel, God is my strength*, would over the years become a reality.

UNDIVIDED
ATTENTION

I WAS A RESTLESS BABY, unable to be comforted. Night-time was the worst. My parents had to sleep in shifts as one would rock me while the other slept, changing places after a couple of hours. When I would finally calm, I was put to sleep between them in their bed. Their warmth seemed to soothe me from 3 AM till around 10 AM.

Father used this time to listen to the radio. On 19 August that year, the Soviet Union collapsed, setting in motion a domino effect, one country after another declared independence. He loved politics, especially since he'd realised that he was missing the Communist Romania. "In what sort of world would my son grow up," he'd say to himself seeing the poverty created by the new regime. "At least everybody had jobs, and you were not afraid to walk on the streets at night."

• • •

My father loved to take me fishing with him during the late afternoons. Those hours of the day were when I was the calmest, as if I was a different baby. The river teemed with fish during late summer and early autumn. He'd leave me in my buggy as he'd put the bait onto the fishing hook. Sometimes he'd hold me with one hand, close to his chest, and with the other grasp the fishing rod. Most of the time he wouldn't catch any fish, but he didn't mind. He was proud to take his son fishing with him.

In the weeks that my father had to go to work, my grandmother came and relieved my mum of the constant work of taking care of me. My cries and shrieks made my mother uncomfortable. Weeks of listening to my wailing awoke something in her from the past. One day, it was my grandmother's turn to rock me, trying to put me to sleep, my mother went to the other bedroom intending to rest for a couple of hours.

Few moments later, she ran into the room where my grandmother was rocking me to sleep yelling: "What if I die now? What shall I do? I feel I am going to die!" Hyperventilating and screaming, she stormed outside barefoot, in her nightgown.

After hours of aimless walking and running in the village, she ended up in someone's back garden.

"Zoe, what happened?" the owner of the house asked worriedly.

But she couldn't talk. Her thoughts were entangled in a torrent of fear, paralysis and irrational thought. The neighbour was kind enough to drive her home.

• • •

These outbreaks increased in intensity and frequency. Most often they'd be triggered when my mother woke up from a nightmare. In the chaos of the moment, she wouldn't realise that she'd left me alone in the house desperately crying. I was vulnerable and abandoned as she aimlessly ran for hours.

These episodes only took place when my father was at the mine. During the weeks that he was at home, mum never had nightmares or outbursts. She'd decided to keep that from my father. Her secret would soon come out, as mum's sister-in-law, who lived next door, told my father what she saw and heard when he was away at work. My parent's marriage began to unravel once he learnt what was happening.

One morning, Mum heard my father talking on the phone with his good mate: "I feel cheated, Emil! I only blame Tiberius and Tim. They never told me about her issues. Her father should have warned me about what I was getting into! That weakling of a man could not admit that Zoe was damaged goods!"

When Mum heard what he'd said, something inside her broke. Darkness engulfed her. She felt tossed aside, like a cigarette butt that my father would throw away, after smoking it.

Soon after that day, she moved out of their bedroom and into the guest room where she would sleep with me, giving the excuse that my father needed the rest. Three weeks after the phone conversation, Dad insisted that she check herself into a psychiatric hospital thirty kilometres away from Cislău, under the recommendation of the family doctor.

The pills the psychiatrists gave her made her dizzy and wiped her mind blank. Hidden somewhere in the maze of emotions, was the feeling of missing me.

She would pace up and down in her minimally furnished room. On the back-left corner was a steel-framed one-person bed and a small nightstand. On the opposite corner, a modest sink and unpolished mirror. The only window in the room was tiny, barred and uncurtained.

She felt thoroughly inconsolable, craving the smell and smile of her baby. She knew she had to get better, or else she could lose me forever. *Help me get better, Lord. I want that fear gone. I need to prove to Radu that I am not weak; I want to be the wife and mother I am supposed to be. Get me out of this place as soon as possible.*

· · ·

I was sent to live with my grandparents for a couple of months. Already able to crawl, *Mămaia*, my grandmother, would let me explore the grassy hills while she fed the herd of cows on a nearby pasture. Already I hungered to probe the world, restless, always testing boundaries.

Tătaia, my grandfather, stared at me long minutes at time as I chased cows and played with their calves. He tried to hide his smile, not allowing himself to feel the surge of happiness. Ever since Christian died, his heart had grown cold. When no one was watching, he'd take my hand into his hand and allow me to play with his rugged fingers.

My uncle Claudiu, who was twenty years old at the time, loved playing with me, throwing me in the air and catching me. He'd parade me to all his friends in the village with a sense of pride he'd never felt before. I was his precious little nephew.

At the end of January, my mother came back home. She hated the cold and the snowy weather, but at least she had me now. She vowed to never risk losing me again. My parents' shared looks began to grow colder, even though my mother moved back into the master bedroom. She'd missed being held, the sensation of protection only a man could give her.

· · ·

Two weeks later, the house was filled with a jubilant atmosphere – my baptism. It started at home, early in the morning with live music, drinking and dancing. In the room adjacent to the master bedroom, *Mămaia* poured lukewarm water with Holy Water into a big copper basin so that I'd become clean. At the bottom there were coins which stood for wealth, and small stones, so that I'd develop into a strong and powerful man. Rose petals, basil leaves and poppy flowers floated on the surface. After the bathing, I was dressed in a four-piece lime white linen bodysuit, longalls, and a bowtie my godmother had bought for the baptism.

Every person outside the house kissed me, then my parents carried me into an ornate cart pulled by two white horses that brought us to church. *Mămaia* held me the whole time.

For the first time in my life, I was brought into the presence of God. For Mum this was her second time in that church. She'd never really been that interested in church affairs, but that day, she was particularly drawn to the imagery inside the building. As she carried me in her arms, as people walked outside, after the service, she heard a voice inside her mind, like a gentle breeze. "You will meet Me one day, through him."

Mum did not know who that voice was, or what it meant. But it did not trouble her either. She forgot about that day, only to revisit it decades later, by accident.

• • •

At nine months and two weeks old, I started walking on my own. From that moment, I could wander even further. My mother would take me on walks into the hills around our house. She'd take a picnic basket with my baby formula, drinks, a blanket, and her beloved fashion magazines. Sometimes she'd just stare into nothingness as I explored every petal of every flower on the grassland, fascinated with the smells, colours and textures. My child-like wonder made her smile. But behind that smile hid her fear of losing me.

Dad did not look at her the way he did before. She'd hear him talk to his friends on the phone about how stuck he felt in the marriage. She did not have the courage to ask him about that. Inside her, she feared him.

Gradually, the handsome man she married two years ago turned into a cold man, removed from their domestic lives. She began craving his affectionate touches, his romantic gestures, his wonderful smile. Love was slowly reduced to duty.

• • •

Fifteen months after I was born, Mum realised she was pregnant again. Mum and Dad decided to build another room onto the house, so that my brother and I could sleep in our own room. During the late stage of her pregnancy, Mum learnt new lullabies. With one hand she caressed my forehead as I was falling asleep, and with the other, she stroked her belly.

They decided to name him *Adrian Christian* because Mum absolutely loved *Adrian* and his middle name was chosen to remind her of her late little brother. Adi's birth was eagerly awaited. At 1:30 AM, on 28 March 1993, my little brother was born. I was at my grandparent's place in Claudiu's care when the phone rang delivering the thrilling news.

Adi's vernix-covered skin was more purple when he came out of the womb and his hands and feet were of a deeper blue colour than usual. When *Mămaia* saw him for the first time, she exclaimed, "What an ugly baby!" My mum didn't react to it, but it cut a wound that she'd carry for the rest of her life.

Mămaia didn't want to hold Adi and she stormed out of the hospital. Mum cried holding her newborn baby close to her bare chest. She loved him with a strength she'd never experienced before, only thinking of her precious little baby.

I soon realised that my place in the bed with my parents had been usurped by this little man. He was very quiet and hardly ever cried. I loved playing with his fingers as he'd squeeze mine in his delicate hand. His forest green eyes would sometimes lock onto my gaze for minutes on end.

• • •

Getting used to sleeping on my own proved problematic for my parents. They'd scream at me when I had trouble getting to sleep.

"Why can't you be as easy as your little brother?" said Dad.

"Look at him! He is an angel, unlike you!" yelled my mother.

Most nights I'd fall asleep crying. Suddenly, all the attention that I'd enjoyed before was replaced by a negligence that stung a thousand times more than a bee.

The next three years of my life I spent mostly at *Mămaia* and *Tătaia's*. Why did I have to be away from my parents for such a long time? I never understood. Claudiu worked most of the time and my grandparents were too busy with their farm, so I was often left on my own to play with the animals in the stables.

I began to understand what loneliness meant. With the mind of a four-year-old, I felt like the only star after the sun went down. I'd spend hours watching the night sky, thinking that they must feel the same way. Somehow, the stars consoled me. *God, if you are there, as Tătaia said, make my parents love me again. I want my mother to hug me, like she used to.*

• • •

At the age of five, while I was spending the summer at my grandparents' place, I got to know the daughter of a good friend of Claudiu's who lived two houses down the road.

We enjoyed playing together. She helped me forget about my loneliness for the months I spent with *Mămaia* and *Tătaia*. If I was not at her place, she would be at mine. She loved singing and gradually I mustered enough courage to sing as well.

I felt that I belonged. Finally I'd found a person who would dedicate all her attention to spending time with me. I couldn't wait for summer, so I could see my playmate and tell her everything that happened since last time we saw each other. Her grandmother loved me as if I were her grandson. She took us with her on her daily summer expeditions in search of lime blossom. When the flowers wilted, women used them as tea.

Up to the age of six, my child's mind had been protected from the dangers and the grime of the real world. I lived in my imaginary universe, discovered with my own hands and feet. But all too soon, that innocence would be invaded.

INNOCENCE LOST

CISLĂU IS A TYPICAL southern Romanian village sitting at the foot of a sub-Carpathian mountain, split in two by the road that connects the city of Buzău to the biggest city in the region – Braşov. Villagers would often gather by the river near the rusty dark grey bridge in summertime.

One of the poorest villages in the county, Cislău had the most hard-working people I have ever known, as well as the coarsest.

The most well-off families, able to afford a television set, became propagators of news to the entire village. The visit of Bill Clinton in Bucharest made some people hopeful of the future.

"Maybe the Romanian-American partnership will take us out of these Dark Ages," said Mum washing clothes by hand. "This way we might afford the things *those westerners* have."

"And bring with them their loose ways?" replied my father. "Was it not enough that our own values changed once this farce they call capitalism took over our country?"

"Our boys deserve to grow up with a better future, Radu! More innovative, more modern, and with the toilet in the house, for goodness' sake, not somewhere in the garden ... freezing your arse off in winter."

"We'll see what your Americans will do," chided Father storming outside.

• • •

Growing up I learnt of an ethnic divide between ethnic Romanians and *țigani*, the derogatory term given to the gypsies. The former, including my family, considered the *țigani* a sub-class. Although they'd been inhabitants for some decades, they were still viewed as outsiders.

I was never comfortable with the way the gipsies were treated because Marta, one of my good friends, and the most beautiful girl I'd ever seen, was a *țigancă*. I always saw her wearing label clothes in a fashionable style. Sometimes, I'd see her wear make-up and do something to her hair that would make me stare at her. "Oh, stop it!" she'd say. "Haven't you seen beautiful little girls before?"

Marta was the daughter of a Brethren pastor, a denomination with a dubious reputation within the Orthodox community in my village. We were the same age and her thirst for discovery appealed to me.

One night, she overheard her father describing to her mother how he saw a man and a woman go into the bushes at a truck stop. He pulled her underwear down and he pushed his face into her crotch.

Marta barged into her parents' bedroom demanding to be told why he did that. "Did she like it, Daddy?" she asked. Her father slapped her cheek. Crying, she ran to her room, locking the door. As she dried her tears, she decided she'd figure it out.

It had to be something very important for her to get punished for only being curious.

One sunny afternoon in the middle of a hot July, Marta told me that she had to show me something alluring. I helped her put a couple of tractor wheels on top of each other and then she invited me to join her inside this black fort. Intrigued, I climbed in. It smelt of stale water and burnt rubber. The inner rim of the wheels imprinted on my back as I leaned against it.

Marta didn't seem at all nervous. Giggling, she told me to remove my shorts. A surge of mixed feelings raced through my veins making the tips of my fingers and ears tingle. Hesitantly, I pulled my shorts down. Then she also removed her own trousers and her underwear. My face was now red. I stood agog.

The next thing she said etched into my brain more deeply than the imprints of the wheels on my back.

"I want you to kiss my *thingy*, Alex!" she demanded. I reluctantly leaned down and gave it a glancing kiss. "You make my mind dance!" she murmured. As I was sensing her enjoyment, I continued doing it until she stopped me. "I want to do the same with you, Alex."

Paralysed, I was unable to move my hands. So she removed my underwear, and began doing the same thing to me. Suddenly, a feeling of shame swelled inside my chest. But I couldn't stop her. She was so elated, looking up at me from time to time. "Do it again to me!" she said.

As I was trying to find a more comfortable position, her older sister called her. Panicking, I grappled to put my underwear and shorts on. Marta seemed unaffected; she calmly pulled her clothes back on. As I was trying to get out of the fort, I heard Marta's sister say: "Alex, your mum is looking for you. She wants you to go home."

. . .

The journey back home, normally only ten minutes, felt like an eternity. Greeting every elderly woman having afternoon tea in the garden, I thought they could see right through me … what I'd done.

I was utterly ashamed. Regardless of the disgrace I sensed every time I tried to relive the emotions Marta had evoked, a window opened inside me, and it beckoned me.

I could not tell a living soul about what happened. They wouldn't understand what I went through, because no one could've ever felt it before. I was a pioneer and a martyr. Marta ignored me for the next few months, but somehow that gave me a sense of peace. I couldn't look into her eyes anymore. After that, we drifted apart more and more every day.

For the first time, I felt the need to talk to my father about what had happened. I desired his embrace and to hear him tell me that I was still his son, despite what I'd done. I needed to know that I was precious in his eyes and that he rejoiced in who I was.

But every time I wanted to catch his attention, he was too preoccupied repairing an old television set or radio, belonging to some stranger from the village. Sometimes Adi would also help him solder an electric capacitor or a diode on an electric board. My father was so proud of my brother. I felt so jealous and I would've given everything just to have my father look at me like that, if just for a couple of seconds.

My thirst for knowledge and my insatiable curiosity kept me sane the year I was six, just before going to primary school. My mother decided not to send us to kindergarten with the pretext that we needed to help her with chores around the house.

I grew up with a number of pigs, chickens, geese, ducks, dogs and cats. So, we all had our tasks in making sure they were well fed and that we cleaned their coops and kennels. But I knew that she just couldn't stand being left on her own.

. . .

When both of my parents went out of the house for a lengthy time, I'd convince my brother to search through the normally off-bounds drawers and cabinets. One day I discovered something that would change my life.

Inside one of the drawers of a sideboard in my parents' bedroom, I found two magazines full of naked women. Flicking through them, it bombarded me with memories of my experience with Marta from months ago. Guilt washed over me. My brother ran away without saying a word. But I lingered a couple of minutes more, turning page after page. There were pictures of men as well. I wondered whether my father also looked like one of those people.

As I put them back into the drawer, I felt anger towards my father. Why would he have such magazines of all those naked women as a married man? Did my mother know? Did they also do those things in the magazines? I knew I couldn't ask them, but I wanted answers.

. . .

The week after my discovery I decided to explore the storeroom adjacent to my parents' bedroom. The walls were painted in an aubergine paled by rays of light blasting through the large windows. A strange acrid odour hung in the air and from time to time I could smell rodent faeces. As I knew I had plenty of time, as the family had gone to the village fair, I stayed at home by pretending that I wasn't feeling well and took my time.

The room was filled with circuit boards, old television sets, broken electronic equipment, and books. In the southern corner of the room stood an old iron stove. One of the doors creaked open. Between the ash and cigarette butts, I found something that looked like an elongated balloon that had a vanilla white liquid inside. After I managed to untie the knot, I tried sniffing what was inside. The pungent smell made me cringe, and after touching it, I realised that it was sticky. A rush of questions filled my mind.

The next day, I decided to go and ask Dan, a classmate I played with sometimes. "Dan, what do you think this balloon is?" I queried reluctantly. When he explained to me what I had smelled and touched, I was disgusted with myself. Once again, a sense of shame enveloped me. But strangely, it made me even more curious. How did that liquid get into the *prezervativ*? Could I also produce that substance? Or wasn't I manly enough?

More than ever, I wanted to share this explorative journey with my father. I wanted him to tell me how come those things ended up in the stove. But for the past months he'd barely even noticed me. He and my brother were building a drilling rig; they were to test whether there'd be a water pocket in our back garden, so that we could have our own water supply.

. . .

Because of my unanswered curiosity about his body, I decided to watch my father bathe. We didn't have a separate bathroom with a bathtub or shower growing up. We had to bathe ourselves in a plastic tub in the kitchen. My mother didn't close the door to our bedroom when she'd take a bath, and that made me uncomfortable and ashamed. I couldn't bear the idea of seeing my mother naked. But I didn't experience the same disgust that night when I watched my father.

When I noticed that he put the big kettle on the stove to boil water, I told Mum that I'd go for a walk outside. I was praying that she wouldn't suspect what I was planning to do.

The kitchen faced the main road and people could see me from the street as I peeked through the small wooden-framed window. But honestly, I didn't care; all my attention was focused on my mission.

Like tasting the forbidden fruit, I knew that being able to see my father in all his masculine nakedness would open my eyes to a world I had, so far, been locked out of. With only one eye, I tried to make out the details of his body through the laced white curtain that adorned the window.

Like witnessing a mythical ritual, I took in every stroke, every movement, and their sequence. I couldn't wait to follow the same steps as he did. I felt no shame. My mother still helped us with the bathing, but she never took so much time to do it.

I knew from that moment on that was how I wanted to wash myself. The way my father did it. I became overwhelmed by this strange desire to be there with him and have him teach me why he washed himself in that order. When he finished, I ran away into the cornfield. Could he have felt my presence?

● ● ●

The summer before I went to primary school, the image I had of my father would change forever. As usual, I would play in the cornfield with my little red Corvette toy car on the sandy earth. The generous canopy of the corn stalks – twice as tall as me – sheltered me from the sun and the absence of my father.

In a couple of weeks, the village would bustle because of the harvest. Almost every family owned a patch of land on which they cultivated corn. After the cob dried, people ground the corn at the local mill – our favourite hang-out during autumn months. We used the flour for making *mămăligă*, a cheap substitute for bread for the coming winter.

Harvest brought families together. Even the youngest children would help with chores. Neighbours would work together to store vegetables and fruits before the cold would paralyse village life. From late August till the beginning of November the streets would buzz with the rattling sound of the wooden cart wheels pulled by horses.

As I daydreamed about the adventures I'd experience this coming harvest, I heard my mother scream; a hellish shriek. I ran as fast as I could into the house only to find my mother wiping tears and blotting blood off her face. Looking at my father, I saw something in his eyes I'd never seen before. I didn't know what it was, but shivers flooded me. I rushed to my mother and helped her clean her face.

Suddenly I felt a blow to my head that threw me on the floor.

"You are just as weak as your handicapped mother."

"Father, why do you beat me?" I said shocked.

"You are not a boy; you are a pathetic little girl. You'll never be a man!"

His words cut through the pain I felt in my head from the punch. It reached an uncharted territory in my heart. A landscape that would, from that day forward, become the foundation on which I'd build my existence as a man. I planted a small seed of hate towards my father into the soil of my being.

As he left the room, the paralysis I felt in my body began to lift, and I slowly regained control over my limbs. The man that I admired so much despite his distance, had just told me that I would never become a man – something that he was himself.

I didn't know what choice I was left with; I was not a girl, even though my mother had called me and my brother "her little girls" ever since we were in her womb. (I hated her for that, but I never had the courage to tell her). That afternoon I became acquainted with a concept that soon would turn into my best friend – self-hatred.

* * *

I spent the rest of the summer mostly doing chores and playing in the cornfield. I hadn't said a word to my father since that day. I simply couldn't look him in the eye. At the sound of his voice my eyes would weep like autumn rain.

I couldn't wait for school to start. I loved the smell of the unmarked notebooks and the inkwell. That first-day excitement was a prelude to a scholastic adventure that would last for more than two decades.

I was asked to sit next to Maya, a talkative and amicable girl. I'd seen her at the kindergarten on the few times my mother allowed me to go, but I'd never had a conversation with her. My shyness oozed from every pore of my body. I couldn't connect two sentences in a logical fashion. (I blamed Mum for my lack of social ability. She never allowed us to have kids over at our house. When I'd spend too much time at a friend's house, she'd ask me to sever the relationship).

I began to loathe the prohibition to show an interest in Maya's life. Like learning a foreign language, the simple act of saying "hello" would make my stomach churn. She showed tremendous patience, allowing me to define myself in relation to her.

One day, Maya said in a matter-of-fact tone, "We decided we are friends now, so there is no need for you to mumble anymore."

"I ... I ... guess ... you're right."

"So, tell me everything about you!" she added.

For the next eight years, we'd sit next to each other in class, she'd become my best friend, sister, confidant, lover. She'd be my oasis when I'd need someone to love me unconditionally. I'd gradually open my heart to her feminine world, and she'd listen to my hour-long rantings. And I was ever so grateful.

• • •

During the first two years school was a refuge from my domestic Calvary. My mother became even more controlling, irritated and dominant. If I moved an object from the place she'd put it, her fury would rise up and she would hit me relentlessly. I couldn't understand.

My father mostly ignored me. I made curls and lines in my notebook, that soon would turn into letters and words, craving his affirmation. When I'd ask him to help me build wooden windmills together for the Creative Minds class, he'd say "Don't bother me with your stupid childish things." I often wondered what made him so bitter.

One day after school, I saw him in the kitchen with Adi on his lap eating my favourite salami, probably bought from the city. I was so excited to taste it again. When I tried to cut a couple slices, Father slapped my hand and said, "This is only for your brother! If you want to eat, you should ask your mother to buy you some!"

His eyes had the same glare as the day he threw me on the ground, and I could smell a whiff of alcohol. My heart broke even further. The seed of hate that started as a grain of pepper, grew into a peach kernel. But I could also feel the fear of him flooding my body. No one comforted me, not even my mother, whose side I'd taken months earlier.

* * *

One evening when I was resting on the couch I saw my mother playing with Adi. Her face radiated with happiness as she tickled my brother. I put my head in between two cushions, and I began crying. I felt like I was in a deep forest, in the middle of the night, with no source of light and heat. My world was imploding; no one was there to save me.

As my sobbing increased, I uttered a muted, "No one loves me." My mother must have heard it, because she drew my head from between the cushions and wiped my tears. She unconvincingly said, "I do love you, Alex!"

I was certain that she didn't mean that. How can one love another person and be so cruel?

* * *

The next two years, up to the age of ten, felt like a movie in fast-forward in my theatre of memories. I only remember feelings of isolation, rancour, despondency and distrust.

As a ten-year-old, I started to notice the emotional and physical distance between my parents. My mother had moved out of the master bedroom, making my brother and I share our bed with her. I felt violated. Our own little masculine corner in the house had now been invaded by my mother's overpowering femininity. From time to time, she'd go up to my father's bedroom for what felt like fifteen minutes in the evening, after we fell asleep. When she came back into our bed, she'd always be sobbing, soaking her pillow with tears.

One morning, when I was alone with her in the kitchen, I asked her why she always cried when she came back from my father's bedroom. What happened next, awakened a whole new set of emotions.

She started complaining in great detail about what my father was doing to her body. For the first time, I realised what the mechanics behind sex were. I made a vow to myself that I'd never do that with a woman. From that day on, my mother would complain to me about her fifteen-minute visitation the night before.

When I was around eleven, I noticed that she didn't go to my father's bedroom in the evening anymore, and this continued up to the moment I moved out of the house, at the age of nineteen.

Having the whole bedroom to himself, my father slowly started to repair broken electronic items there. The whole room was filled with electric boards, parts of television sets, spare parts, welding machines, and other objects he used for his hobby.

The odour of melted resin and solder wire, ethanol, and rusty metals created an almost temple-like experience in the *upper-room*, as my mother called it. Unbearable.

Sometimes, he'd only sleep on one side of the bed; the other occupied by inanimate objects. I couldn't understand his cult-like obsession with accumulating more electronic parts and objects. Adi was the only one allowed to keep him company while he was working. Sometimes, I found myself staring through the window at them, taking in the concentration with which my brother took in every detail.

. . .

In the summer of 2002, Mum started to use emotional blackmail to make my brother and I do things she didn't want to do. She'd send us to neighbours, sometimes without telling them in advance, and have us ask them to lend my parents money. If we refused, she'd say that we were parasites and that we didn't contribute to the household. My brother seemed unaffected by her words, but I felt so guilty that in the end, I'd always go. Sometimes the neighbours didn't want to lend them any money and I'd go home empty handed. Most of the time, she didn't believe that I'd gone, so I'd get beaten. Soon, my anger towards her would turn into hate. Some days I despised my mother so much, I could feel no trace of love.

. . .

The final straw between my father and I happened at midnight in August, that same year. I heard the front door open with a bang and I woke to an intoxicating smell of alcohol. My father stood hovering above me, trying to wake my brother up. "Adi, have you used my bike, today?" he said huskily. Adi uttered a quiet and dismissive denial to which my father replied: "Alright, go back to sleep dear boy!" But Adi had played with Dad's bike that day, trying to ride it for a while in the yard.

The next thing I knew, Dad pulled me out of my bed and dragged me into the cold night air to where the bike was stored. I could hear the crickets chirp in the grass and our neighbours' dogs barking from our neighbours.

My entire body shook, and I panicked.

"Tell me, why did you break the handbrake?" he said angrily.

"It wasn't me. I swear!" I yelled crying.

He punched me with his bare fists, hitting me in the face, chest, abdomen, and torso. One blow threw me to the floor.

He then kicked me in my stomach and head. When I tried to cover my face with my hands, one blow bent my fingers to breaking point. The smell of the bare earth flooded my senses, and in that second I wanted to die. I wished the earth would call me home.

I looked up at him through my fingers. He looked like a monster consumed by rage. He was no longer my father. After a couple of minutes, the violence ceased. I realised that my mother had been screaming at him to make him stop. *If that was Adi*, I thought, *she'd have stepped in to save him from all that pain, but I am not as important to her.*

That night I slept in the cornfield, with a wounded body and a broken heart. It crossed my mind to go to the police the next day, but I knew that he wouldn't be punished; I'd be beaten even more if I did that. I hated my weak eleven-year-old body. I would've loved to have supernatural strength, so I could've hit him back.

•   •   •

My friend Dan and I became quite close, as we travelled together from school on the same road. The two-kilometre journey always gave us a chance to explore new topics, possible futures.

"I can't wait to get out of this poverty-stricken village!" said Dan.

"I'm not sure I ever can. Father doesn't want to pay my university degree, and with only high school I don't think I will get a job in a big town," I groaned.

"You can always become a priest. I see you like going to church," said Dan.

"I've actually been thinking about that. I'd love to be able to travel to other countries, but I'm afraid that won't be in the books for me."

"Oh well, we'll see, eh? Don't be late tomorrow morning!" replied Dan, shaking my hand.

I began to notice that he could afford a lot of food for lunch from the grocery store next to the school. When I asked him where he got the money from, he told me that he stole it from his parents.

I'd never thought of such a thing before, but I knew where my parents kept their money. So, one day when both left to go to the marketplace, I went into the master bedroom and rummaged through the clothes in the wardrobe until I found the place where the moey was hidden. I took the equivalent of a week of my father's pay. I knew he wouldn't notice it, as he earned a good amount.

I felt powerful having all that money. I think somehow, unconsciously, I wanted to get caught. The next day, I went to the local boutique and bought a couple of toy cars. I played with them only when I was on my own in the cornfield. The owner called my parents that same day telling them what I'd bought. They realised I'd stolen from them. I fabricated a lie and they believed it.

My second attempt to get their attention was shoplifting. When I finished school one afternoon, I entered a store in the village on my way home. When I noticed that the salesclerk was busy with another customer, I took a face cream and I put it in my pocket. On my way out, she put her hand on my shoulder, and demanded the cream back. As I slowly took it out of my pocket, she asked me to give her my parents' phone number.

That night I had slept in the cornfield again nursing the beatings I got from my parents.

Afraid of the dark, my mind imagined shapes and sounds. My imagination – so many times my faithful companion –turned against me that night. I could hear noises from our neighbours – the family of my father's half-brother. I knew that my grand-father lived there with his second wife, but my brother and I weren't allowed to make contact. We never understood why.

I reached their front gate, curious; what were they arguing about? Looking through the wooden slats, I saw a frail old man, hardly able to walk on his own. *What if you would have given a darn about your grandkids? Maybe when your son decided which child to love and which to hate I would have had some support. Maybe I would have had your shoulder to cry on, when my wounds oozed pain like the honey from your ruddy honeycombs. We were only twenty metres away, but I guess if you neglected your son, why would you care for us?*

I walked back to my sanctuary with a bitter heart and thick tears on my cheeks. I rubbed my eyes with such vigour that it felt as if I had been using sandpaper, obliterating evidence of tears, and the notion that I had been crying.

* * *

Over the following days, my parents tried to shame me at every opportunity, but their words didn't touch me.

"We have a thief in our midst! Maybe not such a weakling after all!" said my father taunting me.

"Yes, you shamed our entire family, you stupid boy!" added my mother.

"Do you take his side, now? How quickly do some people forget their benefactors," I countered.

"Get out before I make your face as crimson as *those* roses," raged Mum.

For the next few weeks, the conversations between my parents and I consisted of issuing directions. "Do this chore." "Go grocery shopping." "Feed the animals." I tried concentrating on my studies while something inside my heart blossomed. Among the chaos, I was about to experience the greatest emotion of all.

ENAMOURED

MAYA WAS THE ONLY PERSON I talked to about my situation at home. She never tried to solve it; I loved this the most about her. Occasionally she'd give me suggestions on how to temper my behaviour. I looked up to her because of her academic prowess; she was the second best in our class.

Her mother was an art teacher in a neighbouring village. I would have loved to have had a mother like her. I was fascinated by art, especially painting and photography. My parents knew nothing about composers, painting or artists. Though she was a severe woman, she was always polite to me, asking about my health and how my parents were doing. The few times I visited Maya, I felt comfortable in her home.

They had a strange way of incorporating God in what felt like every sentence. They spoke about Him with a sense of awe and fascination. My father always cussed when using the name of God or various saints. Maya's family instilled in me a sense of reverence and a curiosity to learn more about this God they held in such high esteem.

Her father spoke in such a calm and collected way that sometimes I lost my patience listening to his many stories about Jesus and other biblical stories. But his composure and quiet temper made me feel so jealous of Maya. Why couldn't I have a father like him? Some moments I'd find myself craving for her father's embrace, if only just for a second.

• • •

Falling in love with Maya hit me like a sudden lightning strike. I'd always thought she was beautiful, but my attraction to her heart happened gradually. When I was sorrowful, Maya would be the first person I spoke to.

Her femininity wasn't overpowering in the same way as my mother's. She had a fascinating way of engaging her emotions when making decisions. I was always scared of my feelings, which most of the time were so strong, I had no control over them. Maya possessed a weird intuition. She knew how to help me process emotions in a way that was not painful.

Her intelligence also mesmerised me. My parents told me that I was good-for-nothing and dim-witted. Because I never considered myself intelligent, based on the lack of self-confidence instilled in me by Mum and Dad, I was dazzled by the people I deemed to be astute. Maya had a way of analysing a situation that made me want to be just like her.

She was the first person in my life that called out the creative ego in me. I'd find myself writing poetry when thinking about her and the feelings she stirred. When she told me that she was in love with me, my mind felt liberated to explore the multitude of emotions that adults called *dragoste*.

"Why would you love someone like me, Maya?" I asked her.

"Your spirit is beautiful, Alex. All the things you've been going through because of your family didn't darken that

74

wonderful light inside you. You've been dealt a bad hand, but your eyes still smile. That is why I've fallen in love with you."

Maya's words felt like heavenly ointment on my wounds, still bleeding. I framed them in my heart like an icon – an idol of sorts that I'd worship when the people around me reminded me of my worthlessness.

• • •

One day as we were sitting next to each other in class, I gave Maya a ring I'd made out of textile threads. After I put it on her ring finger, she stared into my eyes for what felt like a million years. Her glance reached my eyes like summer rain on drought-scarred soil. I imagined my entire future with her as my wife. I was overwhelmed with emotions. For the briefest of moments, I held her hand for the first and last time.

In the weeks and months following our 'marriage' ceremony, we were inseparable. I couldn't pay attention in class very well, and I could no longer focus on my homework. My notebooks were filled with fragments of poetry and rhymeless verses. After school, I'd accompany Maya for a while on her way home, creating our own story and planning the future.

Some days we'd go to the train station in the village and spend hours talking. I was fascinated by trains and railways – probably a reflection of the strong desire to go places my imagination failed to conceive.

The walls of the station were graffitied with coarse words and obscene images. With my twelve-year-old mind, I believed that what I saw represented the village itself – uneducated, uncouth, poor, and uncultivated.

"I want our children to grow in a better environment, Maya!"

"You will be a wonderful father, Alex! Don't worry!" declared Maya.

"What if I make the same mistakes my parents made with me? I'm afraid, Maya. I really am."

Maya took me in her arms, and simply said, "Your heart is made to become a father, Alex. There is so much love inside it for so many people. Trust me if you don't trust yourself." As we headed back to her home, I looked back again. *Lord, please get me out of this village. Show me the world.*

* * *

Maya slowly started to distance herself emotionally and physically from me. Without giving a reason, she told me to stop walking her home, and refused to be seen with me in the schoolyard during breaks.

I began questioning myself more than ever. Wasn't I as intelligent as she had thought? Did she now find me boring and uninteresting?

A few weeks later, I saw her with Dan, my classmate who lived near my house, giggling as they held each other's hands. Betrayal flooding my body turned to disappointment and culminated in despair.

It didn't make sense. *Why would she hook up with Dan, my friend? I thought things were going so well with us. What if she tells him secrets about my family? I'll be in such trouble. Just like my mother, another woman telling me that she loves me, she ended up hurting me even more.*

Maya's rejection exacerbated the need to be seen, loved and accepted. At the same time, I shut people off. But soon, I'd meet someone who would open my heart anew – reaching new heights, and deeper levels of pain.

ANATHEMISED

IN THE SUMMER of my thirteenth year I met Cezar, who'd moved to our village with his family from Bucharest. He was five years older than me, and his younger brother, was two years younger.

Cezar's brother was an energetic and cheeky boy with whom I clicked immediately. We shared the same passion for discovering the world and an insatiable curiosity to know as many things as possible. My mother wasn't happy that I was spending so much time with him. She wouldn't allow me to bring him home, so I spent most of the time at his place. We'd climb every tree we found and run through the meadows until our legs gave way.

Cezar would only join us when we played *de-a v-ați ascunselea*, a Romanian version of hide-and-seek. He was a tall lad, quite muscular, with a beautiful smile. I enjoyed his sense of humour and the feeling of safety I experienced when I was with him. He had this almost mysterious aura that made him seem distinguished, sophisticated, and a bit unreachable. I made it my mission to get him to see me. *If I could get close with someone like Cezar, then I must be good and lovable after all.*

• • •

The first time he brushed my shoulder with his torso while playing football, my entire body felt electrified, as if I'd touched a god. From time to time, I'd catch him looking at my body. I thought nothing of it.

One day he invited me to go with him to a market in a village thirty kilometres from Cislău; he wanted to buy a new pair of football boots. Out of all the kids he knew in the village, I felt honoured that he'd asked me.

The marketplace – a hundred-metre open-air alley with stalls on either side –overwhelmed me with its smells, faces, colours, and sounds. A deafening cacophony of *Manele* – gypsy Middle-Eastern songs – blasted from new cassette players.

Cezar walked at speed; it was difficult to keep up with him. I was out of breath, but I didn't mind because for the first time in a long while, I felt needed and valued. I was beginning to allow another person into my heart.

When he reached the stall with the boots he was looking for, he asked my opinion; which colour and model would best suit him. Someone had finally noticed me. Like being exposed to the gentle warmth of the sun for the first time, my spirit blossomed. I found the friend I was looking for.

• • •

The next evening, when Adi, Cezar and I we were playing *de-a v-ați ascunselea*, Cezar followed me as we searched for hiding spots. He was suddenly behind me, startling me, but I was happy he was there.

We crouched down so Adi couldn't spot our heads. As I was trying to get comfortable, my hand brushed his for a fraction of a second. Normally I'd have paid no attention, but that evening something brewed. A shiver flooded my body like liquid lightning.

He looked deeply into my eyes, smiled and held my hand. "Don't tell anyone about this," he said abruptly. A second later, he left to find another hiding spot.

That night, I couldn't sleep. New feelings rushed through my mind. My lower body started to react and that shocked me. I didn't know what to do; I couldn't talk to anyone about it.

Unable to sleep, I went outside and looked at the stars. I wondered whether Maya's God existed. Did He really care about me? If He was indeed a father, how could He allow my parents to make me suffer like this?

The tears on my cheek suddenly felt icy, and I realised how cold it was. Looking up I felt that millions of stars sang my name through their twinkling. But their song had an ominous rhythm. *Does it have anything to do with what happened this evening?*

•   •   •

The next evening, Cezar followed me again to my secret spot. As we sat close together, he touched my leg. The feeling of his hand on my bare skin awoke the electricity inside me until it overwhelmed me. As his face came closer to mine, my breathing stopped, and I felt myself blush. As happened with Marta, a strange paralysis took over my body. "Don't resist, just trust me; I wouldn't do anything to anything to hurt you," said Cezar, disarming my fear.

As his lips touched mine, his hand stroked my neck, caressed my ear. At that moment my body had no resistance. But then shame stalked behind the feelings of elation and bliss, like a skilful hunter. As his tongue brushed mine, I pulled away from his grip and ran away. I was engulfed in this feeling of darkness, shame, and regret. Thoughts of Maya came to mind, and my desire that she'd be the first person I wanted to experience that type of kiss with.

After an hour of running, immersed in myriad thoughts, I stopped at the edge of a forest, near where my mother took me on our picnic trips. This was where I first learnt to walk, where I discovered what natural beauty was, the place I was loved.

My thoughts had been screaming only one word ever since I fled the scene with Cezar: *poponar*, a derogatory term I heard my father use, referring to one of his colleagues who was caught kissing another man. He then went on to say: "That dog is the scum of the universe. No one should be friends with him anymore."

Was I also like that man? Was I also a dog that didn't deserve to be loved? As I returned home, I noticed a puddle on the road. My reflection glowed in the light of the starry night. *Is my soul as ugly as my distorted face reflected in this muddy water? What have I done?*

● ● ●

I was determined to bury the memory so deep that no one could unearth it; not even myself. I couldn't bear the thought of being someone or *something* my father abhorred. I began talking to Maya's God. I was so angry that He'd created someone like me. As I tried to structure my thoughts, tears streamed down my face. Soaking wet, I arrived home, changed my clothes, and went to bed saying no word to Adi or Mum.

I was sure that Cezar wouldn't try to kiss me anymore. He

couldn't risk being known as a *poponar*. He had much more to lose than me. I decided that night to never speak of it again.

. . .

As it was still pleasantly warm outside, that late August 2004 summer, my brother decided to organise another games evening, inviting Cezar and his younger brother. My palms sweated profusely, and my heart raced.

When it was time to hide again, I choose another spot. My mother had decided not to keep a pig that year, so I picked the empty sty in the back garden; the perfect hiding spot.

The hay that kept the pig warm last winter before it was slaughtered was still heavy with urine and faeces; in the summer warmth, it was overpowering. I could still see the coagulated blood on the decking where he was stabbed to death. I hated that ritual, the sight of blood and the squealing just before the pig died. I'd always go to stay with my grandparents a week before and a week after my parents butchered the pig.

As I was trying to think of something else, I heard someone outside the sty. I thought my brother had finally found my hiding spot. But it wasn't my brother. Cezar stood in front of the door of the entrance, smiling. He came in and touched my face with the back of his hand. When he came closer to kiss me, I tried pulling away, but I could not; his hands were glued to the sides of my head.

I couldn't escape his grip. He started to get undressed, slowly pulling down his trousers and his underwear, standing half naked with an evil smirk on his face.

He forced me to look at his genitals. Suddenly, he forcibly pulled my face into his groin, telling me to open my mouth. Barely able to speak because of my lips being blocked by the skin of his scrotum, I managed to say, "I don't want to do that! Leave me alone!"

Releasing my head from his grip, he looked into my eyes and told me, "If you don't do as I say, I'll tell your father that you tried kissing me yesterday!"

"But that isn't true!" I cried.

"I know he doesn't love you. Do you think he will believe you when I will tell him that?" said Cezar.

Blood rushed through my veins like a supersonic train. I could feel my face burning with anger. I hated myself for not being able to stand up to him. But I was more afraid of my father. I knew he'd kill me if he was told that I was a *poponar*. A couple of months before, he'd said to me and my brother that if we ever didn't obey his commands, he'd kill us, and if he was sent to prison, then he'd etch images of us on the wall of his prison cell with which to remember us by.

I knew I had no escape; it was either this or getting killed by my father. When Cezar tried to force me again, I didn't resist him. I could barely stop the urge to vomit in between the gags. The smell and taste of urine and the choking sensation of his genitals in my mouth made me feel as if someone was trying to strangle me.

Eventually, he stopped and asked me to remove my trousers and underwear. I didn't want to do this, so I tried to break free. But as I tried to stand, he caught hold of my trousers and he pulled them down by force. He thrust himself inside me. The pain I then felt was alien – of a different quality than anything I had experienced before – emotionally intertwined with hopelessness and violation.

As my body ached with unbearable pain, something inside me broke apart. I lost myself in a darkness so dismal, I couldn't find any humanity left in those parts of my soul. With every thrust, he pushed me deeper into an ocean of self-hatred.

After a couple of minutes, my tears ran dry and through my sobbing, I felt a warm sensation inside my body. I realised he must have ejaculated. A couple of seconds later, he vanished.

I stayed there, half-naked, for what felt like a lifetime. Devoid of thoughts and emotions, I rested on the wooden decking, my broken body soiled with Cezar's semen, pig's faeces, and urine. An unfamiliar voice shouted in my head, "Alex, you are now officially a *poponar!*" And I believed it. There was only one place I could go.

* * *

The sun had already set when I jumped into the river. We were prohibited from swimming at night, but I didn't care. The compulsion to wash out the squalor consumed me. As the water cleansed the semen off my skin, I looked towards the starry sky. The twinkling stars weren't calling my name anymore, but a silent "*Alex poponarul.*" I realised that not even Maya's God loved me. If He did, He could've stopped Cezar.

I arrived very late home that night. Mum screamed at me, demanding to know where I'd been, but I could barely pay attention. She slapped me, but the pain of her hand was like a gentle breeze after the hurricane that had swept through everything an hour before.

* * *

In the months that followed, I walked around in a state of limbo. One day I saw Cezar's mother and as I looked at her, I felt a deep hate for her. What she then said stung like a wasp the size of *Betelgeuse*. With a demonic grin she asked: "What is it boy, did Cezar not stuff your butt well enough?"

My nails nearly pierced the skin of my clenched palms. I wanted so badly to punch her face so she could feel the pain inside me. But I couldn't move, or utter a word. She knew what her son did to me, and she was proud of him.

The spark inside me had faded. The light I was looking for in the world would soon be replaced by darkness.

THE
OTHER REALM

MY MUM'S PANIC ATTACKS RETURNED. In the middle of the night, she'd wake up from a nightmare and would start screaming, convinced she was about to die. My brother would wake up terrified. As I was trying to comfort Adi, I felt I also needed to reassure my mum that she wasn't going to die.

Usually she forced us to follow her wherever she'd go in the middle of the night, poorly dressed, sleepy, and confused. One night we ended up across the street, in the garden of an elderly man who always made me feel uneasy.

As my mother knocked on the door, dogs barked frightening my brother even more.

"What are you doing? You cannot just wake someone up, in the middle of the night," I said pulling her hand away from the door.

"I don't have any choice, Alex. I'm scared!"

"And what do you think about us? Look at Adi ... he's terrified," I replied annoyed.

As I held Adi's shaking body in my arms, my hate towards

Mum grew inside my spirit like ivy. The elderly man seemed distressed as he opened the door. After a short exchange of words, he asked us to come into the house.

The fusty smell awoke my slumberous mind and body. The only source of light in the room came from a couple of logs burning in the wood stove. The shadows cast by the flames made the man look like the monsters in my comic books. Opposite the fireplace I could see a single bed and a small wooden table. He asked us to lay down on a hard sofa.

My brother had fallen asleep, with his head on my shoulder. My mind started wandering through the deserted place of my heart. I felt alone, scared and burdened with the responsibility of taking care of my brother; Mum seemed to be unable to do it herself.

Before I knew it, I'd fallen asleep as well. It was still dark outside when I felt a hand on my shoulder shaking me awake. Mum whispered that we needed to go back home before the sunrise. She didn't want the neighbours to see us coming out of this man's house.

• • •

Her outbursts were so frequent that I dreaded going to sleep in the evening. Even though I hated my father, wishing him gone, when he was at home for two weeks, we could at least sleep in our own bed for the entire night.

I felt so uncomfortable as a fourteen-year-old having to sleep in the same bed as my mother. Why could she not go and sleep with Father? My brother and I swore that we would never disclose that secret to any person in the world.

• • •

One Saturday morning, as I was waking, I heard loud voices coming from the kitchen. I could hear my mother laugh, but I couldn't make out the other voice. After I got dressed, I decided to go and check.

It was the village witch. Growing up, I'd heard stories of her hiding little *draci* underneath her bed – demons and other demonical creatures. When my brother and I passed by her house, we'd always make the sign of the cross to protect ourselves from the power of the evil that we thought resided in her home.

Seeing her in my house, my heart raced and my palms began to sweat. She greeted me with a grin directly from hell. Something rather weighty began to form inside my spirit as she tried to make small talk with me. Her eyes looked dead as she locked her gaze with mine. My mother sensed my discomfort, so she asked me to go to the grocery store to buy some coffee for her mysterious guest.

• • •

In the beginning, the witch visited mum once a week, but after a couple of months, she was at our home almost every day. I began having terrible nightmares, and my days were shrouded in agitation. I suddenly couldn't control my anger, and the hate I had buried in me would spurt every time my mother or my father would do something awful to me.

The only place that calmed my soul was the willow tree on the bank of the Buzău river. With my feet touching the fast running stream, I oftentimes thought of jumping in the current. *Life would be much more untroubled for my family if I ceased to exist. But what will meet me, at the end of death?*

• • •

I started to have a recurring nightmare. I'd find myself trapped in a windowless house made of cardboard blocks. The diffused light cast otherworldly shadows on the uneven walls; an eerie tune played over and over again.

I stepped on the putrid pulp of the plums, so vivid, real, and frightening. Every nightmare would end with me finding an open door at the back of the house. As I stepped over the threshold, about to get outside, a faceless shimmering being would appear in my face. The eerie tune would stop, and the walls would melt away. As my heartbeat increased to bursting, the faceless entity started screaming. My being would be drenched in liquid fear; I felt I was drowning. Bit by bit I saw the life inside of me ebbing away. Just before death touched the bottom of my spirit, I'd wake up. Awake, next to my brother and mother, I could always feel the presence of the entity lurking in the room. For a couple of seconds, I'd still be paralysed, physically and emotionally.

As the nightmares' intensity increased, I started seeing shadow-like apparitions after the sun went down. They'd lurk in dark corners of the house and in my hiding spot in the cornfield. Once my sanctuary had been invaded, I had no other refuge around the house.

As I was lying in bed trying to fall asleep, I could hear the furniture squeaking and the sound of footsteps in the ceiling. The fear was overwhelming.

• • •

Paradoxically, I felt noticed, seen, and that gave me a certain willingness to live, again. I was taken over by this desire to know more of the previously unseen reality. So, I decided to ask the witch about her experiences with her little creatures.

One Tuesday afternoon I agreed to visit her, after having been invited a couple of times before, but never having taken up the invitation. At the end of a very long and narrow corridor, I could see a walnut brown door without a doorknob. She pushed it open and after I entered the room, the door closed by itself. I was startled and when she noticed this, she reached out and took my hand, with the same evil smirk she'd given me months before. *She probably always knew that I was going to visit her shrine.*

With no windows, the room was dark, the only sources of light a small red light bulb inside a round material globe hanging off the ceiling. The smell inside was similar to burnt clothing. Even though this was a very noisy part of the village, I couldn't hear any noise once inside.

Trying to be cool, I sat at the table, its tablecloth impregnated with old vanilla wax. The witch took a pack of cards from the table and began to shuffle. As she chanted a song – that sounded like gibberish – my shoulders began to feel heavy.

My mind felt like it was being poured into a glass. As I lost control over my thoughts, the weight on my shoulders lifted; I felt light, ethereal. I could still see her shuffling the cards and her chanting. Suddenly, she began talking to me. Her words sounded like a song without a tune. I couldn't understand what was happening. I felt the hair of an animal brushing over my legs, sending shivers all over my body.

As she told me things from my past she couldn't have known, I felt engulfed with the desire to know how to do that myself.

Would I be allowed to chant the conjuration like her? Would I be able to read someone else's past?

As the fear lifted, I sensed time flowing like a frozen river streaming through immovable rocks into a gorge. While the tuneless music coming from her words entered my mind, I grew addicted to the sensation. Looking closer at the face-up cards, I saw the painted characters on them, mostly sinister looking. How could they tell her things about me that I'd never shared with another living soul?

The mood changed. I began to feel like myself again, as the atmosphere returned to normal. It ended abruptly, like a badly scripted movie. She led me back to the hallway, towards the front door. On each side wall were pictures of albino young men in their early twenties looking down. A quick shiver crossed my body. As she noticed me staring at the boys, she gently pushed me towards the door. Out in the street, I couldn't believe what I'd just experienced. *I need to learn how to predict the future. Maybe I can finally escape this wretched reality.*

I kept what happened a secret. I knew no one would believe me and I couldn't bear the thought of being seen as a freak. But when I was on my own, I would search the internet for how to conjure spirits. A new world opened in front of my eyes. Spread through the country, hundreds of conjurers and sorcerers promised to teach me how to become like one of them.

●　●　●

One month after my meeting with the witch, I decided to apply the knowledge I had learnt from the conversation with a crystal gazer from Iași. After I'd drawn a pentagram on the ground, in my front garden, I placed myself in the lotus position in its middle. I chanted numinous words over and over again, as instructed.

The daylight around me began to fade as I repeated the incantation. I felt I was being eaten away by this overpowering presence – stronger than any of the others I'd felt and seen before – encircling me like a colossal tornado. Bit by bit, my mind was consumed by a darkness incredily real. Chunks of audible words assaulted my ears, as if someone threw living pieces of jig-saw puzzle at me. My tongue made sounds unknown to me, as I slowly forgot who I was.

Suddenly, piercing through all the sensations in my body, I could hear Mum calling my name. The darkness lifted, and the evil presence fled my body and spirit. As if waking up from an anaesthetic, I could barely say the words "Yes, Mum!" I was thankful beyond measure for her interruption.

. . .

I'd been playing with forces beyond my imagination and power, and I decided to stop searching the internet for occultism and conjuring of *draci*. *But if these creatures that I thought were myths truly existed, then their good Nemesis must also exist. What if Maya was right all along?*

The nightmares continued with more frequency. I felt haunted during the day by this entity. My concentration in school dropped drastically, and at home I almost became invisible. From the young boy who'd find it challenging to contain his energy, I became lethargic and absent. I had no energy to even play with my brother.

In the middle of my struggle for understanding, Maya made contact.

We met on the bank of the river.

"I am so sorry, Alex. I don't know what had happened to me," said Maya.

"Did he break up with you? That is why you came back to me?" I spat, unable to contain my anger.

"No, Alex... My heart wouldn't let Dan inside it. I still love you... I always have," said Maya with tears in her eyes.

"Your rejection hurt so badly, Maya. Still does."

"I know. I am sorry. Let's start again. I swear in front of your special tree that I will never leave you again. Okay?"

"Alright. But you'll have to have patience with me," I said, losing myself in her eyes.

A few months after that, she became part of my life once again. She'd soon bring someone into my existence who would change me forever.

CRUMBS

EVEN THOUGH WE STARTED TALKING with each other again, I wasn't the same person anymore. Maya was still a gorgeous young woman, and every time I looked at her, my heart would skip a beat, but my body didn't react like it used to. I'd cry myself to sleep trying to force myself to fall in love with her again, but I couldn't.

I began feeling attracted to men who visited my father for business. Because the door between our bedrooms was tinted, I could stare for a long time at the clients in Dad's room without being noticed. I longed for their embrace, their attention, and their masculine energy. Some evenings, when my father would drink *țuică* with his friends, I loved to eavesdrop on their conversations. I craved to be part of their masculine world.

I'd want to see them naked, so curious about the shape of their bodies. I'd feel incredibly ashamed, but the desire to be touched and loved was stronger than gravity itself. On a Sunday evening, when Father usually had the most visitors, I was listening outside the door to their stories about their sexual adventures on the drilling rig. It wasn't very hard for me to imagine the details.

Mum caught me, as she was getting ready to go to bed.

"Why are you spying on them like a little rat?"

"I was just listening. I find their stories interesting," I whispered, trying to hide my excitement.

"They are just telling drab stories to each other ... stupid men," my mother blurted disgusted.

Her words cut through my defences. I could see she had stopped hiding her hate for my father. Did Mum hate me as well, for being a man? Was that why she called me *fetița lu' mama* – mamma's little girl?

. . .

One day, as I was coming back home from the local store, I noticed a man from afar who went underneath the bridge near my house, to relieve himself. The desire to see him urinate, consumed me like the power of the igneous July sun. My dad never wanted to be seen naked by us.

One autumn afternoon, when my brother and I went fishing with him, I almost got caught trying to see him pee. That same desire impelled me to spy on the man below the bridge. I would've given anything to just have a glimpse, to have a sense of intimacy with him. I felt like a freak.

The internet provided a sense of solace. I could see everything I longed for. But the thing I desired the most – being loved and touched by a man – I couldn't get. The profile of the men I was looking for on the internet embodied most of the characteristics of my father: always much older than me, hairy, muscular, and hypermasculine. The transient comfort and bliss offered by masturbation became my addiction. I was obsessed with getting my fix every time I felt alone, rejected and inadequate. And those needs demanded sating daily.

One day, I rediscovered my father's pornographic magazines in the drawers of his nightstand. They were the same ones I looked at years before. One picture had been engraved into my memory for many years after that day – rugby players having a shower together after a match. I noticed that the female bodies weren't attractive to me anymore. I was drawn towards the male bodies in different scenes.

• • •

Carrying this secret on my own wore me down. With every fibre of my being, I wanted those desires to be taken away from me. I wanted to tell Maya about them, but I didn't want to lose her again. *No one would like to talk to a poponar, Alex. You will have to carry that weight yourself.*

Maya had big plans for her life. She wanted to study art and literature in Bucharest. I admired her ambition and discipline. Her paintings were absolutely fabulous. I loved encouraging her and giving her ideas about what to paint next. In return, she always pushed me to write poems and fuel my curiosity by exploring the world around me.

Our conversations had become even more centred around her God. Ruminating about my experience with the unseen entities convinced me that because they were real, Maya's God must exist as well. But no matter how curious I was to go to a church service in Maya's church, I knew my Father would kill me if he heard.

If you were a *pocăit*, a person belonging to a Protestant church, you were considered by the Orthodox population a half-Romanian. If you converted from Orthodoxism and fully became a *pocăit*, you became a traitor of your culture, identity, and country. My father's views about this were even stronger, saying that someone abandoning the true faith for a cult, ceased to be a human being.

. . .

Because of the fear I felt for my father, I'd decided to seek this God that Maya was talking about in the Orthodox church. One beautiful late April afternoon I told Mum I wanted to go to *denii*, a church service that took place every evening during Lent in the Romanian Orthodox Church.

That morning I picked some anemone from a meadow a couple of kilometres from home – it was traditional to bring flowers for these special church services. The fruit trees alongside the road to the church were in bloom, giving off a wonderful sweet fragrance.

The village buzzed. Grandmothers walked hand-in-hand with their grandkids, festively dressed and carrying colourful flowers. Like under a spell, everybody smiled, being unusually kind to each other. "Who's that young bloke?" I'd hear people whispering to each other behind me. "He's Radu's oldest. We haven't seen him before." Ignoring the chatter, I tried to channel my thoughts into discovering a sense of divinity in that place.

The frankincense filling the church reminded me of the séance with the village witch, but this time the feeling wasn't tinged with fear. A sense of peace and mystery filled every painting that adorned the walls.

In the middle of the church a table was filled with the flowers people had brought that late afternoon. As I put my bouquet on the pile, I looked up for a brief moment. Painted on the dome, Christ was depicted looking down, with his arms wide open as if inviting someone for an embrace. His eyes were kind and His welcoming smile made me grin briefly. He felt familiar.

After the service, I went to my paternal grandfather's tomb for the first time. He had already been dead for two years. Anger invaded my thoughts, and it paralysed the happiness I'd been feeling that evening. I hadn't forgiven him for not wanting to have a relationship with my brother and I, even though we lived on the opposite side of the street. I was jealous of my cousins who had got to know him. But mostly I was angry at him for not giving me the chance to learn about beekeeping. Their industriousness and beauty were fascinating.

• • •

I loved the magnetism of that place of worship. I felt at peace during the church service and the mystery of the liturgy fascinated me. The chants uplifted my soul, and for the duration of the service my thoughts weren't engulfed in the ever-present darkness of the past five years.

I decided to walk outside before bed every night after that *denii* evening and tell Maya's God about my experiences. I didn't feel that I was talking to a real person, but I revelled in voicing what was happening inside me.

• • •

My mother became even more irascible. Her raging outbursts made me cry even before she would hit me. The anticipation of pain made me shiver like I was freezing. She looked as if she was inhabited by an evil spirit, crawling out of her eyes – just as she was about to let the fury consume her.

One day, she went to visit my grandparents, having given us clear instructions about our chores. It was a beautiful beginning of March, the plum trees were in bloom and the land danced in the gently warm sunlight of early spring. On the eighth, we celebrated Mother's Day. Every child would give their mother a *mărțișor* – a self-made talisman adorned with a red-and-white string with hanging tassels – that was believed it would bring the wearer strength and happiness for the rest of the year.

Mum decided to give her own *mărțișor* to *Mămaia* even though she had second thoughts.

"I don't like this hypocrisy of looking so happy to see her, when in fact I don't. This day reminds me of what a terrible mother she was to me ... still is!"

"But you know she'd like that," I said, trying to convince her to go.

"You better do what I told you. Take care of your brother."

We decided to make our own *mărțișor* for her out of thin copper wires we found in Dad's shed. Adi used Dad's soldering gun to put the intricate pieces together, while I painted them with red paint I found in the shed. Intoxicated with the fun we were having and the anticipation of surprise we'd see on Mum's face, we forgot about the instructions she gave us before she left.

When she came back later, she realised that the animals were still unfed. Her eyes glazed over with fury and she grabbed the first thing she saw – the blade of an old chainsaw. The teeth of the blade pierced through our skin. When I noticed Adi's skin turning salmon pink, I panicked, and ran away. She'd stepped on the beautiful butterfly we worked hours to solder, paint, and make special for her.

My back burned, the pain was unbearable. I wiped my tears away thinking about leaving home; I couldn't put up with her anymore. Seeing my brother in so much agony devastated me. I could take it, but I knew he wasn't as strong as me.

Because I still had a couple months left before I could go to high school, I decided to stay. I wanted to study economics at the Colegiul Economic in Buzău, and that would give me the break I'd been waiting for. Because the high school was thirty kilometres away from Cislău, I knew I'd have to live on my own in the city, away from the pain and sheltered from my mother's rage.

* * *

Those last months of secondary school crawled as if the Creator had pushed the slow-motion button by mistake. The total eclipse of the Sun, on the eleventh of August was the only thing that kept me excited. Father gave my brother and I his welding mask, so we could document the mysterious event.

My journal was full of sketches I had made days before, inspired by an atlas I'd found amongst Dad's wiring diagram magazines.

"It looks just like when you bite a cookie, Adi!"

"Lemme see," said my brother, snatching the welding mask from my hand. "Whoa! What was that flash?"

"That is what the book called the 'diamond ring effect.' That thin circle that you can see at the edge of the Sun is called a 'corona.' That shimmering represents the 'Bailey's beads,' probably after the guy who named that phenomenon," I replied, full of happiness at being able to share this experience with Adi.

Once the Moon moved away from the Sun's disk, I retouched my sketches and added new observations. Dad gave me a furtive look, just enough for me to feel his scepticism about me knowing so much about eclipses. His mistrust stung me for a second, but being part of something bigger than myself helped me forget.

. . .

The prom at the end of my final year of secondary school in Cislău arrived like a hurricane forecast on the weather channel – I knew it was coming, so I could prepare emotionally, yet it hit me harder than expected.

Mum and Dad argued that they had no money to buy me a suit like my other classmates, so I felt like a fool dressed in my black denim jeans and Dad's ridiculous black leather vest. When I entered the ballroom in the community hall, I could sense from the barely concealed sniggers, the disdain my classmates felt for how I was dressed.

I wanted the Earth to swallow me. *Why did I bother coming?* Upon scanning the room, my gaze interlocked with Rosa's. The malice in her eyes had a familiar quality to it – it reminded me of my mother's. Half-a-year ago, she vowed that she'd kill me that night.

"The earth is cursed because of your pathetic *poponar* existence," she said when no one was around in the classroom.

"Who told you that?"

"No one needed to tell me, you piece of scum. I could see it in the way you looked at the boys in the playground."

"It's not …"

"Don't you dare deny it! I will liberate you!" she said in a sinister tone.

As if I had been talking to the Angel of Death himself, I was engulfed in terror.

Tonight, her smile betrayed her true feelings of disgust

towards me. I knew that behind that deceitful grin lay a desire to see me dead.

"A last meal before your long-awaited execution?" she asked, handing me a plate with potato moussaka.

"I am not afraid of you, Rosa!" I stuttered, trying to hide my real feelings.

"I will see you outside, pink little bunny!"

I could not swallow the food and I gasped for air. Just as I moved closer to the open window, Maya's hand on my shoulder startled me.

"You look as if you've seen a ghost," she said smiling.

"I think I did. I want to get out of here. Would you like to join me?" I asked.

"But you've just arrived. What happened?"

"Nothing, I just feel I don't belong here … it's like I'm in a room full of strangers."

"Why do you keep on looking at Rosa?" Maya asked.

"Nothing, she was just looking for trouble. She must have had too much țuică. Can we please go?"

"Alright. Let me get my coat."

* * *

Maya made the whole evening more bearable. I took her to the riverbank, next to the willow tree. I felt so angry with myself for being seen as such a freak that Rosa would want to kill me. I could not tell Maya; she was the only person who made me feel like a normal guy.

During those last four years of secondary school Maya had been my closest friend. No one had wanted to talk to me during recess. I'd felt so abandoned when I'd see my classmates play together after having told me that I wasn't welcome to join them. I couldn't understand why they didn't like me. *Everybody will abandon you eventually, Alex. Eeeeeverybodyyyy.*

Drowning in my ocean of bad memories while staring at the shimmering flow of the river, Maya's voice sounded like an echo carried on the wind, "I will always love you, Alex ... don't forget that. Even if the entire world abandons you, I'll still be there, holding your hand. We are soulmates."

That night could've ended tragically. But Maya's love gave me hope. I haven't seen Rosa since that night. Like a nightmare that one tries to blot out, I slowly began to forget the hate, the disgust, and her threats of death.

• • •

The climax of the pain inflicted on me by my parents happened weeks after the prom, and it would shatter my entire existence.

LOST AND FOUND

BEFORE GOING TO HIGH SCHOOL, my relationship with my father was virtually non-existent. He'd grown old. Walking hunched and wearing worn clothes, he was now just a shadow of the statuesque man he used to be. His bitterness, however, still reined over each conversation we had. No matter what I was doing, it was never good enough.

My brother adored spending time with my father repairing broken TV sets. I could hear the giggles and jokes from my bedroom. I couldn't understand the conflict of feelings inside me; I would've loved to have the same relationship with my father that Adi had, but at the same time, I hated him with all my being.

One day that summer, I mustered the courage to ask him why he never loved me. I needed to know, so I could shut down any hope of having a relationship with him. His reply would change my life in ways I wouldn't have foreseen. He simply said: "You are just like your mother: stupid, impulsive, and good-for-nothing. I wish you were never born. I provide for you because I am obliged by the State, but not because I love you."

The tears built like a torrent storming my eyes, but I held them back until I was out of his sight. I didn't say a word, I simply looked him in the eye for a couple of seconds. A plethora of emotions rushed through my being. I'd never felt a deeper rejection. Like searing a wound, his words wiped away the last fleeting desire to have any connection with him.

My father died for me that day. From that moment on, I've struggled to refer to him as my father to another human being.

I could no longer deal with that level of rejection. I had no idea what to tell myself to be unaffected by what he had told me. Was I so repulsive that not even the person who brought me into this world could love me? Because my emotions were at war inside me, I couldn't control my reactions, most of the time. My brother suffered the most because of it. We argued every day, and sometimes we even fought, then I'd endure more beatings from my mother for upsetting Adi.

• • •

A few weeks after that, Mother had asked me to weed the plants in the vegetable patch. It was during a heatwave, so I told her that I wouldn't be staying in the heat to do that.

"Do as I say, you ungrateful bastard!"

"If you don't want to go because of the heat, why should I do it?" I barked.

"Because I'm your mother and you shouldn't talk back to me."

"And because you are my mother, you should also protect me … don't you think?"

In a rage she declared: "I wish I'd aborted you! I raised a snake at my bosom!"

For a couple of seconds, all I could see was my mother in a white hospital room, being offered the pill that would postpone the appendix removal operation. Instead of swallowing it, I could hear her say: "I don't want that *creature* inside me, I don't want *it* to live!"

I ran away to the bank of the river where I washed myself after Cezar had abused me. I loved the tranquillity; the stream of the water synchronised with the rush of my own thoughts. That day, my mind raced a million times faster than the river. The willow tree that had become my confidante for the past years, couldn't help me.

I could see the bridge in the distance. Built during the Second World War and a landmark in our village, its towering presence beckoned me. Taking step after step towards the top of the bridge, the light inside me began to flicker as if the oxygen was evaporating.

Mindlessly climbing up the metal megalith, the thought of no one loving me weighed me down like a mountain. Reaching the top, I could feel the gush of wind and heat brushing off my cheeks. Looking down, I could see the sharp-edged rocks smiling at me, inviting me to jump. What was I living for? My parents had told me that I shouldn't have been born and that I was not loved. Maya didn't want to be in a romantic relationship with me. The guy that I thought wanted to be my friend, had used my body as if it was just an object. My brother was the only one I still loved.

Feeling rejected, abandoned and alone, I decided to curb my pain and suffering. Images of hell flooded my senses, as my existence felt increasingly worthless. I could almost smell the stench of my skin burning, but it did not hurt as much as the pain I felt inside me. After all, I was trading one hell for another.

As I lifted my right leg so I could build momentum, a voice inside my head suddenly said: "Don't jump, Alex! I've a big plan for your life! I love *you*!" Like a slow-motion film, I gently pulled my entire weight onto the iron beam on top of the bridge.

Like recognising a famous singer's voice on the radio, I knew that Maya's God had just engraved His words in the depths of my being. It was hard to believe that He'd love a *poponar*, a son rejected by his parents, someone so stupid. How could He have a big plan with someone like me? But as I climbed down the bridge, I felt a small seed of hope had been planted in the soil of my heart.

Thereafter, my mother would only communicate with me through my brother. It irked me, but I knew any desire for a relationship with my parents died, falling on those sharp-edged rocks from the iron bridge. They were both dead to me. I wanted to tell them that they almost caused my death, but I was too afraid they wouldn't care; I couldn't risk another rejection.

● ● ●

On the first day of high school my family didn't want to join me, so I watched alone, as my classmates laughed with their families before the opening ceremony. My father had said the previous day: "My father didn't come with me when I went to high school, so why should I come to your opening ceremony?"

I fought back tears like a martyr before the lions in the arena. *Who will shield me from being seen as a freak? Who will comfort me when the school workload becomes too heavy?*

My classmates were complete strangers to me. I craved the

energetic look in their eyes – the sort of energy that makes people want to learn, exploit their creativity, take on the world, powered by the knowledge that their family loved and believed in them.

Seated in class, the smile of a classmate in front of me pierced through my shield. She seemed genuinely interested in my life and what I'd done until that moment. In the following months, I made other acquaintances who would make my time in high school a little more bearable.

*   *   *

My room in the dorm looked like a long rectangular box with bare ecru painted walls. Four beds stood against the eastern wall and four on the opposite side, divided by a narrow walkway. Because I'd arrived first, I chose the bed near the window, but a block of flats opposite blocked most of the sunlight, making it quite dark.

The first night, while I was asleep, my body was thrown into the air, then thumped onto the cold concrete floor. A thousand laughs broke out around me. This was my initiation as a new student. Part of that induction was surviving the first night, when the beds were turned upside down while *bobocii*, the initiated, were sleeping.

I tried to fall back asleep, but I couldn't. I felt like an alien in this new world. Everyone seemed to have already made deep connections, except me. Not dealing well with the feeling of being on my own, I decided to move back with my parents. I hated the idea of living with them again, but I wanted to have a sense of stability and control, no matter the cost.

The move meant having to commute from Cislău to Buzău by train. Waking up in the morning at five so I could catch an early train was very difficult. I'd arrive at eight-thirty in the city, but my first class wouldn't start until twelve in the afternoon. Most days, I killed time in an internet café talking to people from all over Romania on Yahoo Messenger or playing video games.

I discovered the wonder of being connected to the wide world. On the first of January 2007, Romania became a member of the European Union. I loved reading about the polarised opinions of the West, as well as of our own politicians.

Something about the notion of having a unified Europe thrilled me. I could already imagine my business travels around the continent. My childhood dreams of being able to be a citizen of the world suddenly seemed possible.

• • •

I loved my classes in high school. Marketing was particularly interesting; I could design logos and mottos for the companies we were inventing. I felt affirmed when my classmates were impressed with my ideas. For the first time in a very long time, I rediscovered my passion and curiosity.

Sports class was the toughest. The masculinity of the team paralysed my thoughts. I felt like an impostor in their tough and energetic world. The coach was like a father figure to all of us, forty boys. I thought he was incredibly handsome. I'd stare at him from a distance for minutes, inhaling his masculinity like the salty smell of the ocean. Sometimes, on my trip back home on the train in the evening, I'd imagine him hugging me as we were watching the sunset on the iron bridge in Cislău. I longed for his hands to caress my face and hold my hand, telling me that I was a good person. I would've given anything just to feel loved and accepted by him.

. . .

The other commuters on the train looked unhealthy and dangerous. So many men carried knives and other weapons. Most were trying to sell drugs to easy prey like me – kids that were curious to experiment with narcotics after having been sheltered from them by their parents. The mobile phone black market was another thing that brought them on the night train. College students would buy cheap phones from other kids and sell them to these mobsters at a higher price.

One night, as I was talking to a regular commuter, a thirty-something-year old man took a seat next to me, while another one of similar age sat next to the person I was chatting with. My heart began to race faster; I could feel the pulse in my neck. The guy next to me said ominously, "What is the time?" Because I wasn't wearing a watch, I took out my Nokia 3410 and told him that it was 9.30. As I was trying to put it back into my pocket, the man wrenched it from my hand, and began to look through my messages.

When I tried to get it back, he clenched his hand onto my jaw, and looking straight into my eyes he said, "If you don't stay quiet, your mother will clean your blood off this floor tomorrow morning." His glance carried a weight, as if years of pain had scarred his soul onto the inside of his eyes. I noticed a crescent moon on his left cheek. The whiff of alcohol, bad breath, and the stifling feeling of terror paralysed me for minutes.

Then he took the sim card out of the phone and threw it on the floor as he ran outside, jumping out of the train, which had just pulled out from the station. His other friend stared at me for a second or two as if almost expressing regret, and he left slamming the door between the two carriages of the train.

• • •

I hated myself for feeling so vulnerable, so weak – just like my father had told me. I had no one to protect me from this cruel world; I just knew I had to change. I had to look tough by adopting a false persona. Not knowing who I was anyway, playing a fake version of myself didn't bother me that much.

That experience had taught me of the evil outside my home, even if it didn't hurt as much as my parents' words and punches. Weeks after that, I spent time on courtroom benches because my father wanted to sue the guy who had stolen my phone. We received countless threats from his family, known in the region for their criminal history.

The desire to be dead plagued my thoughts in the first year of high school, especially during the second semester. The voice of Maya's God that promised me a good life was fading with every passing day. I didn't know how to deal with the craving for male intimacy and friendship.

• • •

After crying myself to sleep one night, I dreamt that I was watching television with my brother, laughing about a joke on TV. I then felt compelled to go outside, and though it was a dark night, I could only see a few stars through the thick clouds. The crickets chirped ominously, muffling the barking dogs.

As I tried to figure out what I was looking for, the sky opened, flooding my garden in a diaphanous light. Coming down on what looked to be a pair of hands, I saw a human-like head, hair whiter than anything I'd seen, his gaze piercing my being like millions of needles.

As I tried to focus on him, I had this strong sense of not feeling worthy to look him directly in the eye. Panicking, I went back inside. My brother and the furniture had disappeared. On the sill of a small window sat a leather bag which I hastily prised open. It was full of narrow strips of paper painted in a language I didn't recognise. Strangely, I could understand the meaning of the text.

When I had finished reading the messages, I went back outside to find that the face was still hovering in the air. Hesitating, I looked up again, and said uncertainly, "Now I am ready for you!" I woke up with a deep sense of confusion and astonishment.

• • •

The next day I called Maya to ask her what she thought about my dream. She was adamant that her God was trying to communicate with me. In real life, on that windowsill, my parents had a Bible they received as a wedding present from a family friend. So, we agreed that maybe His message would be in the text of that Bible.

In the following months I became captivated by the Old Testament. It contained a side to this God that I hadn't heard or seen before. The patience He had with Adam and Eve and their offspring amazed me.

I was particularly drawn to His relationship with Joseph – a young Jewish man who had been sold by his brothers to slave masters, taking him to Egypt. He was forced to live in a foreign country, without his family, not knowing anything about this new culture. I felt I understood his situation well.

Later, when the text spoke about the ten plagues that befell

Egypt, my heart began to open its gates to this God that I always thought was too cruel, too distant, too fatherly.

I read tens of chapters per day whenever I could find some spare time. I'd never been an avid reader, but this book made me want to know more.

* * *

One evening, as I read through the first book of Samuel chapter 17 – the story about David and Goliath – I felt the desire to experience God the same way David did. I had made a rational characterisation of Him through my readings, but I wanted to know who He *really* was; feeling Him with my senses.

I had Yanni's *Truth of Touch* in my headphones playing on repeat. The melody transposed me to my sanctuary next to the willow tree. With my eyes closed, allowing my imagination to create the mental space, I said shyly, "God, I want to feel You."

"*Alex, I am always with you!*" said a wind-like voice.

"Is that You, God?"

"*I am,*" the voice added, enveloping me in the most wonderful peace I had experienced – it felt like silk and it smelled of the earth after rain. "*Trust Me, Alex. I will never abandon you ... I love you, son.*"

The word *son* pulled me out of the vision. I couldn't think of God as a father; not yet at least. My Dad had distorted that image to such an extent that I couldn't emotionally dissociate the violence, the hate, its overpowering force.

When I opened my eyes, the tablecloth moved, as if someone had rushed past it. I smiled and allowed the vision to sink into my heart.

• • •

Reading the Bible would soon lead me to meeting people who would impact my life so dramatically, that it would be radically transformed.

ENCLASPED

AFTER MY PHONE WAS STOLEN, I decided to commute to school by bus. It was much more expensive, but I'd be much safer not travelling with the same delinquent passengers.

Having read so much from the Bible already, I realised I had so many questions that needed answers. Without expecting to be heard, I'd been praying for someone to talk to about the mysteries I had discovered in my reading. Though Maya was very patient with the trillions of questions that came her way, I needed someone with more experience and authority.

One winter morning, at the beginning of a long week, I met Nicu, a bus driver. When I stepped into the bus, I was welcomed with a genuine smile and a warm *"Bună dimineața!"* His face radiated a peace and enjoyment of life I'd never seen before.

Concentrating on the drops of rain gliding down the windows, I heard Nicu talk to a passenger about God and His mercy. I heard a voice like thunder saying, *"This man will provide answers to your questions!"* My prayer had been heard.

● ● ●

For the following weeks I made small talk with Nicu, eventually mustering the courage to ask him about the things I didn't understand. He asked me to sit next to him and I absorbed the attention he gave me like a sponge.

In the handshakes I could feel his soft but strong hands, a feature that I could see reflected in his character, gradually getting to know him. That day I decided to slowly test whether he'd be willing to have a religious conversation with me.

When he mentioned he wasn't an Orthodox Christian, I panicked a little, but he assured me that he was talking about the same God. I wasn't sure I believed in anything at that moment, but I was willing to explore this new reality colliding with my life. I was fascinated about his patience in answering every question, even the ludicrous ones.

Day after day, Nicu began to pierce the walls I'd built around my heart. His masculine energy felt like summer rain after years of drought. His attention felt unconditional, and freely given. His light grey hair and smiling eyes strangely reminded me of the image of *real* fatherhood I had envisioned over the years.

One evening, just before I was about to step out of the bus at my stop, he said warmly: "Alex, it would be great if you could come to my church one Sunday!"

"Would I be allowed, if I don't know whether I already believe the stuff you do?"

"Yes, of course. It is God's house …of course you are allowed. That would make me so happy."

"Okay, I will think about it. Thank you!"

I closed the bus door with a wide smile. He seemed to love his church, and him inviting me in their midst electrified my thoughts.

His invitation haunted me for the rest of the week. If my

parents heard that I went to a church belonging to the *pocăiți*, they'd punish me severely. But something inside me tried to convince me to go, despite the risk. The church was in Nehoiu, thirty kilometres away from our village.

The very next Sunday, I decided to lie to my mother, telling her I was going to visit a classmate in Nehoiu. Surprisingly, she didn't question me; she simply said, "Don't make it too long as you'll have to help Adi chop those logs, if you want to have a warm room tonight."

I'd never been to that town before. The cold mountain air filled my lungs with a surprising freshness. Fascinated with the breathtaking scenery, I slowly took in the view as I walked towards the church. Nicu had told me that it was a two-kilometre walk from the town centre, and that I'd have to climb a rather steep hill at the foot of the mountain. The houses looked bigger and well-maintained. The people I met on the way greeted me with a welcoming smile – something I hadn't seen in my village.

The sound of the flowing river calmed my nervousness as I walked along the road to the church. Approaching the building, I could feel my heart beat with every step. Was God going to talk to me again, like He did when I asked Him to reveal Himself to me? Would I be welcomed by the *frații* ['brothers' in Romanian, Nicu used this term to refer to the members of the church; a jargon new to me at that time]?

The building was unpretentious; more like someone's home. Inside were two rows of pews, divided by a wide rosewood coloured carpet. The minimalistic front of the church featured a sturdy light beechwood pulpit. On the walls verses were painted in a powder blue shade. The absence of icons and the smell of frankincense gave the atmosphere an unfamiliar allure.

Nicu looked elated when he noticed me during the service. The simplicity of the liturgy and the honesty in people praying aloud reached my soul with an amazing force. I felt at home.

After the service, Nicu gave me a hug and introduced me to other people, as his friend. It felt like a family reunion, getting to know extended members of a family that I'd never met. They all seemed genuinely interested to get to know me, powered by a sense of affection that I'd never experienced before. "It is so good to have you among us, Alex," seemed to be the chorus of my interaction with them.

In Nicu's embrace I sensed my essence interlocking with a transcendental world. The affection that I'd craved all those years was now partially fulfilled by a man who was able and willing to love me.

Another man at the church introduced to me that day – his name was Luca. I saw in his eyes kindness and a genuine desire to be part of his life. His sermon to the church was brutally honest, vulnerable, and life giving. For the next two years, I'd often be invited to have lunch with his family after church.

"Alex, you are part of us now," said Luca smiling. "I hope you can make it again next week."

"I'd really like that. I'd have to see how my parents will react."

"We will all pray for you, Alex. We have been praying for someone like you."

I did not know what he meant, but I embraced the affirmation-rich words entering my palace of thoughts.

• • •

When I arrived home, I decided to tell my parents about my desire to continue going to church in Nehoiu.

"I thought you said that you went to see your classmate!" said Mum, visibly irritated.

"I know, but I was convinced you wouldn't let me if you knew," I countered.

"I can't stop you, but I don't think your father will allow you."

"Allow him what?" said Dad coming into the kitchen.

"He went to a church of the *pocăiți* this morning," said Mum sarcastically.

"If I hear that you get baptised, you won't live under my roof anymore!" He replied without even looking at me.

I was pleased to see that he didn't forbid me from going. I regained the spark of curiosity and excitement – I gained a new family, one that loved me. I could not wait to see them again.

I began writing poetry again – most of it while listening to Yanni's albums and inspired by what I was reading in the Old Testament. The poems had a different quality to them. They were written about someone I began to fall in love with – the One who saved me years before and who began to conquer my heart with His love.

*　 *　 *

Being able to afford the trip each Sunday would be problematic. However, in the end, numerous members of the church offered to pay for my return ticket each time. Some Saturday evenings I'd wait to hear whether anyone from the church could pay for my ticket and I'd worry that I wouldn't be able to go the following Sunday. But to my astonishment, the money always came through. During the two years of going to *adunare*, the term used for a Protestant church, I missed only one Sunday, and that was because of illness.

Four months after my first day in Nicu's church, I spotted a worn brown Bible on one of the rugged pews. Inside it, I found a piece of paper entitled *The Sinner's Prayer*:

Dear God,
I know I'm a sinner, and I ask for Your forgiveness.
I believe Jesus Christ is Your Son. I believe that He died for my sin and that You raised Him to life.
I want to trust Him as my Saviour and follow Him as Lord, from this day forward.
Guide my life and help me to do Your will.
I pray this in the name of Jesus.
Amen.

After I'd read the text, I realised my cheeks and my shirt were wet with tears. I decided to read it out loud once again, as instructed on the bottom of the page, as if I was talking to Jesus face-to-face.

I could feel a deep sense of tranquillity as if my soul was being slowly immersed into an ocean of liquid peace. The weight on my shoulders that I'd carried for so long was lifted. Seeded in my spirit, was an indescribable desire to live my life. I felt alive.

I began reading the Bible with even more fervour. From the New Testament, I absorbed every word from Jesus' mouth. His relationship with God the Father was so special; I craved it. I wanted to be part of the harmony that existed between Them. I loved Jesus' interaction with the people around Him and the attention He gave to those asking for help.

His masculinity was so different from the manliness I'd observed growing up. He embodied a sense of vulnerability in the way He related to people; a sensibility that was charming but always paired with a strength that wasn't overpowering.

Before getting to know His character, I thought masculinity was always this uncontrollable and tyrannical force that caused pain and hurt. I wanted to learn how to model His personality and spirit.

One morning I was reading the passage that spoke to me the most – the account of John about Jesus' arrest in the Gethsemane garden. I found myself in a vision, hidden behind a tree when I saw Judas coming with the priests from the Temple and a band of soldiers.

Jesus was surprisingly calm, as if He had expected this. The flickers of moonlight reflected in His eyes in a sinister dance, echoing the chorus of a funeral song. The mob's lanterns and torches blinded my sight for a while.

I could see Judas giving Jesus a kiss on His right cheek. His eyes were dark, as if no soul was behind them. He then stepped back, not looking the man he'd just betrayed in the eyes. Just as I was about to give voice to the feelings Judas' actions elicited in my heart, Peter drew a sword and cut the ear of one of the servants of the high priest.

"Put your sword away, Peter. All who take up the sword will die by the sword," said Jesus quietly.

He then covered the priest's severed ear with His right hand, whispering something I could not understand, and the ear grew back. The soldier witnesses were astonished – they looked ashen.

Jesus seemed so collected, so calm, so strong. His divine wrath could have obliterated the life of every soldier, but instead He let them take Him.

Just as He was taken away by the mob, Jesus turned around and smiled. "*I do it for you.*"

When I opened my eyes, I could hear my essence singing for joy.

• • •

My decision to get baptised came naturally. I felt a very strong desire to publicly declare that I was a follower of Christ. Even though I was concerned about how my parents would react, I knew the life I'd discovered was worth it. I finally belonged to a family that loved, accepted and appreciated me. The God that Maya had described became my God.

On 16 August 2011, all dressed in white, I stood poised to dip my feet into the water, surrounded by people who were proud of me for taking the next step. For a few seconds, I imagined my family seated in the pews, radiating happiness for me. I still longed for my father's affirmation. That day was one the happiest days of my life.

On the bus home to Cislău, I still grappled with the concept of grace; I knew rationally what it meant, but I needed to feel *what it was. Father, please show me!*

As I stared at the world outside the window, my eyes began to see another reality. I was in chains, naked, and dirty. Around me were other men like me, whimpering and frightened.

It looked like a market – men and women were passing by, analysing us from head to toe. An elegantly dressed woman stopped in front of me and after she had a close look, she spit at me and went on further.

It was an auction. I was a slave.

In the crowd, I spotted a man dressed in a white robe coming towards me. As He wiped my tears with the back of His hand, my chains melted away. In an instant, a shining robe covered my naked scarred body. The man embraced me and whispered in my ear, "*This is grace.*"

Coming back, I began laughing uncontrollably. I could see

heads turning back towards me, but I didn't mind; I finally understood what grace was.

* * *

My contentment was soon shattered when my father heard that I'd been baptised. Full of rage he told me: "From this day forward you're no longer my son!" His words felt like arrows missing the target, though. A year before I would've been deeply affected, but that day I left his presence with a sense of independence and peace.

The chaotic atmosphere at home became more bearable thanks to the friendships with people from church and the internet. This new online world made me feel like a global explorer. I was able to connect with people from all over the country and beyond. One day, I saw a comment on a forum from a guy called Marin. After a brief exchange of messages, we realised that we could become good friends.

Marin was the second person in my life who recognised my artistic personality. He had a special way of bringing that out of me every time we talked. Soon after, I'd listen to the music he'd recommended, and this became my muse when I wrote poetry. I translated the love that I was discovering from getting to know God into hundreds of verses that I wrote during class.

Through my relationship with Marin, I started to realise how self-centred I was, and how much I desired to be seen. He was patient and he'd listen to my soliloquys for hours. He helped me gain self-confidence and made me realise that I could create beautiful things. I was beginning to accept that I wasn't the good-for-nothing my parents had me believe.

One Saturday afternoon, as I was writing a poem, I saw an

email from Marin. It looked like a short essay – he called it *Weekend with a Poet*:

"Alex …
He is a changed man. He writes now.

He turned the page of his life not long ago, and I could say he started re-writing it, along with the art he discovers within himself and everywhere around him.

At first, that rhymeless, rhythmless, and weird verses he calls 'modern poetry,' got my attention. I knew those literary ideas are somehow brilliant. I could never think of creating many of them, so I sank deeper into knowing him more, so much that now getting to meet each other was a wish both for me and for him.

I promised to myself to try and understand his kind. I wish I could be a 'way out' for him, somehow, and not just for him. I could feel lucky for having him as my friend.

The moment we were going to meet was not so promising, but things changed on our behalf.

I was looking for him with my eyes, in a crowded place, filled with people stepping out from their buses. It was that day we were finally getting the chance to meet. I turned and there he was – the first eye-contact.

He was afraid to smile but eager to give me a hug. I was in a hurry, so it happened fast, I don't remember saying "Hey, how are you?"

I've been his online friend, his listener, reader – almost one year now – talking and sharing life.

I can still see the non-conformism in his bright green

pants. He always has a way of seeing colours, accepting colours, wearing colours... colours that only kids might enjoy. I guess there is a kid in all of us.

For him, everything could be a writing muse. His seventeen-year-old mind could always see more than our eyes just... see. We've had moments when I just couldn't figure out what he's looking at. That's him – unexpected, mysterious, or just being himself.

Apparently, a lot of things I like, or just think about, for him are just ... things. Not easy to impress him, but not hard to share new things I hold on to, like music, cuisine or just opinions.

He likes seeking special things in this simple world, mixing words that people consider literary wrongs, creating something out of nothing and pouring them on the paper.

We spent almost three days, sharing thoughts, beliefs, cultures, arts, perspectives. It felt as if our worlds had collided. All I know is that the Internet brought him into my life, his talent brought him into my attention, his friendship and devotion quickly made him a close friend.

I made a note these days about how special people can be recognized by the way they say their first 'Hello.'

He is one of them."

I cried after reading Marin's essay. For the first time in my life, I had no reply.

• • •

The summer of '09 was fraught as my father convinced me to go with him to Bucharest for two months to help him install new electrical systems in newly built homes. Though I was nervous, I wanted to prove to him that I could support our family.

We found lodgings in a dorm run by a friend in a dilapidated neighbourhood of Bucharest. We were told that we'd share the living room, the kitchen, and the washing facilities with twenty other men, and sleep in the same room with six former colleagues of my father.

Our bedroom was a tall cube – six-by-six metres – painted in a light pear green shade. The room had no furniture, apart from bunk beds. Cluttered with stuffed plastic bags and suitcases, the room tasted of stale and fusty air. Climbing up to the upper bunk bed, a sense of protection surged through my spirit. All these men around me, felt like an invisible masculine embrace.

• • •

Suspended in the air, in those windowless concrete boxes, I had a three hundred and sixty degree bird's eye vista of the entire city. I was just another person, a number, a dot among almost two million other dots. As if possessed by another persona, I took the mobile phone out of my pocket and I started taking photographs of angles, parades of drunken men on the busy streets at night, people having a coffee on the terrace, people in the bus – too exhausted and drowned in their thoughts to notice the young man with concrete-dust-filled dungarees taking pictures of them.

Documenting my life this way felt like living in a parallel reality in which I could finally dictate the next turn, the next tide, the next smile. Behind the paraffin-soiled glass, life looked worthier to be lived, and with a click, immortalised and offered like a sacrifice to my capricious hurting – like a child who promises to stop crying if he gets a candy.

I became proficient at it, like being able to speak a foreign language after having been immersed in the culture for a while. Once I had the courage to share my photographs, people's reactions became my opium. The more pictures I took, the more I felt alive, the more I was seen.

• • •

I wish I could have paid more attention to Mum's cooking. Rather I learnt how to like canned food. A varied diet consisting of beans-on-toast for breakfast, kebab sandwiches for lunch, and canned soup with almost-fried mackerel for dinner, being the only thing Dad knew how to cook. Some evenings, we decided to diversify with something called 'Lasagna De La Lupu' – a Pisa-like tower of undercooked pasta sheets glued together by a sauce resembling Frankenstein's clogged blood. I'd look at it for a long while, until I became so ravenous that the hunger numbed the blandness of my small and unconvincing bites.

Despite the fun we had making food, working with my father caused a lot of sadness and frustration. Nothing I did was ever good enough. Tony, a forty-something year old guy from Cluj, noticed me suffering in silence and tried to console me by taking me out for walks in the evening. He was tall and had a strong build, giving me a sense of protection walking through the dark and eerie neighbourhood.

"I also had a father like yours, Alex. There were other times, then ... I couldn't talk to anybody about the way he treated me. Don't isolate yourself," said Tony.

"There are moments when, if I could, I'd take a pill to erase myself from this earth."

"I know, I had similar thoughts … but you know what? I can see in you a capable young man, who despite the tragedy and the misery, turned out to be a polite and sensible person. Prove him wrong, Alex."

Not knowing how to deal with the compliments, I simply asked, "How can I prove him wrong, Tony?"

"Be stronger than him by not allowing his remarks reach your heart. Deep inside you, you know what your father's telling you isn't true."

"I'll pray for it. I have to believe that God cares …"

I became addicted to spending time with him. For the first time in my life, I contemplated a parallel reality in which Tony and I loved each other. I felt a certain repulsion as I pictured this – a sense of shame and self-hate. But at the same time, the desire to be utterly vulnerable with a man, to be completely seen and yet loved, was so powerful, that sometimes I felt I needed it more than oxygen.

• • •

At the end of summer, just before I returned to Cislău, I gave Tony a quick embrace. I felt as if I'd inlaid pieces of my heart into his bright yellow shirt. I've never forgotten his sweet gaze hidden behind the azure blue eyes. His kindness and willingness to listen to me during those evening walks helped me believe I could withstand the malice coming from Dad.

Once we arrived home, I went to my place in the cornfield. The salty taste of my tears combined with the sweet smell of the ripe September corn felt like my magical memories of Tony entwined with the fact that I was alone again.

My connection with God had weakened during the months I worked in Bucharest. Seeing everyone back in *adunare* in Nehoiu and receiving their love, gave me impetus to focus on my relationship with God again. Praying became much easier. My favourite moment of the day was in the evening when I could see the stars twinkling. Just like when I was a child, I thought that their sparkle was their special Morse code, telling me that I was loved.

Admiring their celestial dancing, I loved composing good-night messages on my mobile phone, that I'd send to Nicu, Luca, and other friends from church. I allowed my creativity to run wild through the landscape of my thoughts, making unusual connections, but always coming to the point of wishing them a restful sleep under God's care. Unconsciously, I wanted to receive a message back, a spark of gratitude that someone thought of them, or in fact, me receiving a speck of attention. Attention overdose; oh, how sweet it tasted.

● ● ●

When I turned eighteen, my father said to me, in a creepily happy tone: "I am no longer forced by the State to provide for you; you'll have to earn your keep from today on."

I was on my own. My mother would've wanted me to stay home, to continue playing the role of a substitute husband, confidant, stress-reliever, and heaven knows what else, but our relationship was so strained, I sometimes thought I'd go mad. I couldn't see at that time the toxicity of our bond – a bond she weaved with the sorrow of her doomed choices and the hurt of a rejected daughter who was wished dead by the woman who brought her into this world.

One day, a couple of months after I'd come back from working with my father, she was so engulfed with rage, that she raised her hand to slap me. Like in a slow-motion film, I grabbed her arm and suspended it in the air.

With a calmness I'd never mustered before, I looked deep into her eyes and said: "This is the last time you will raise your hand to me."

I could no longer tolerate the way she made me feel for all those years: emasculated, infantilised and fragile. She retracted her hand and left the room hastily, as if she had seen a ghost. The child she'd been calling "my little girl" all his life became a young man.

I wondered whether that was the defining moment in my life as a man.

Like a guest who has overstayed his welcome, I knew it was time to start a new life elsewhere. I needed a place that I could call *home*, a word as foreign as happiness itself. Soon, my appetite for exploration would bring me to shores that I never knew existed.

SPROUTS

EXODUS

MY DESIRE TO LEAVE my parents' house became like a song that gets stuck in one's mind. Having graduated from high school, the free time I had was becoming my enemy. I knew I'd do anything to get me out of the village.

A few weeks before the start of summer that year, my prayers were answered. A friend from church, Laur, suggested that I could join him for a project on a farm in a German village outside Munich. Laur explained the type of job I'd do, but I ignored the details, all the while feeling the cage around my heart loosening.

Like the restlessness of a teenager in love, I couldn't wait for the day I'd fly for the first time. Up in the air, a few weeks later, I knew my existence had been directing me to that point, launching me beyond the limits of my domestic life and crossing my country's borders.

It felt as if I was on a different planet. The roads, the houses, the billboards, and the people looked so alien to what I was used to seeing. The ground had dried out after a week of torrential rain, but the atmosphere retained the rawness of the downpour, trapped between the leaves of the lofty green trees.

Reaching the farm, I couldn't feel prouder of myself. I wandered around the estate for a couple of hours, taking in the vastness of the agricultural land. Tall trees acted as a natural boundary, enthroned between the sky and the vastness of green wheat, marrying them in a beautiful symphony of colours.

"*Velcoome* mister *Loupou*," said an elderly man in a heavy German accent, who would turn out to be my employer.

He led Laur and I to the back of the farm through countless stables and poorly lit corridors. I noticed little German flags in the corners of the rooms we passed through – most likely an aftermath of the FIFA World Cup that had just finished.

"*Zehr* you go!" said the elderly man, showing us a vanilla white caravan.

"*Vielen Dank!*" murmured Laur, nodding his head slightly in acknowledgement.

We slept in the two-berth caravan, equipped with a kitchenette, Laur's bed at the end, and mine close to the door. A refreshing draught through the window cooled the air inside. Old German newspapers taped on the window next to my bed with yellow duct tape acted as both isolation and privacy, probably stuck up by previous seasonal workers.

As Laur meticulously took his clothes from the suitcase, he folded them and arranged them by colour on the shelves next to his bed, I took a surreptitious photograph of him silhouetted by the evening sunlight coming through the open door. I giggled as I noticed the flickers of light dancing on his bald head.

"Are you nervous about tomorrow?" he said, breaking the silence.

"I'll have to admit that I am. I've never done anything like this before, so, I'll have to learn on the job."

"You don't have to worry ... I'll be there with you to help you and teach you what to do. You look so much like my boy. You could be brothers."

"Thank you, Laur. Knowing that I'm not alone disarms some of my anxiety.

• • •

The next day we started demolishing an old farm building, so that the owner could construct another corn silo. Laur reassured me that he'd help me every step of the way. As I looked up at the old concrete building – larger and taller than my own house back home, I was overwhelmed by the daunting task, but Laur's trust in my abilities helped me cast away the fear. "I will be there with you and help you," was the mantra I repeated in my head over and over again.

The first week on the job proved exhausting. By the first weekend, my energy was too depleted to explore the surrounding area; I just wanted to sleep. In the end, I decided to accompany Laur on the weekly grocery shopping expedition, only to find myself even more emotionally and mentally drained.

Not being able to express myself in German was challenging, and for the first time I got to know other people through someone else's interpretation.

"*Ich bin ein Hamburger,*" said the boss one morning, helping me with the sledgehammer. "*Wo in Rumänien lebst du?*"

"What's he saying, Laur?"

"I think he wants to know whether we eat hamburgers in Romania," responded Laur, laughing.

Laur tried to say in his best German that we do, in fact, love hamburgers. Months after I came back to Romania, I realised that the boss told me that he was coming from Hamburg. I cracked up laughing and couldn't wait to tell Laur about it.

• • •

The evenings, when we bathed before bed proved to be the hardest for me. I'd savour every moment I could see Laur undressing before going to have a shower. Like in a theatre of disparate forces, pleasure and guilt paraded before my eyes.

The chiselled shape of his body had the same gravitational force as the reverberation of the primaeval feelings inside my heart; just like Adam wanting to touch the forbidden fruit, I desired to trace every depression on Laur's body. I was scared that he might see me staring.

My pulse raced and I could feel its throb in my throat as if I was falling to earth on a skydive. In fact I was falling – in love with the way Laur made me feel.

• • •

Handling the demolition hammer began to take a toll. After a couple of hours of drilling into the impenetrable concrete, my hands would give way. So Laur had to work even harder to achieve the quota for us both.

The fear of disappointing him began to overwhelm my emotions. After only three weeks of working on the farm, I felt like a nuisance, a weak boy who couldn't prove to his father that he was a man now. While the phantoms from the past slowly persuaded me to believe that I was indeed good-for-nothing, another distinct voice enticed me into going back to Romania.

One morning, while I was smashing through the concrete slabs, I accidently cut off the tip of my thumb. The gush of blood and numbing pain transported me back into my father's workshop when my mother raged with a chainsaw blade. Only this time I was alone. I listened to a voice in my head that confirmed that I was not suited for the world of men.

"Alex, please hold on for a while longer … give it another two weeks. It will get much easier once your strength builds up," Laur pleaded.

"I can't do it anymore Laur, I am not cut for this kind of work," I replied, regretting the words as they came out of my mouth.

"But I promised I'd help you. I think I did …"

"You have and I am incredibly grateful … I really am. I just *know* I won't make it. If not now, in a couple of weeks we will be debating the same issue."

"It is your choice, Alex. It is a shame to throw away such an opportunity … Your choice," said Laur, leaving the caravan.

• • •

On the way back to Cislău, praying was my only consolation. I didn't know how to face the disappointment waiting for me at home.

Neither my mother nor my father said anything about me coming back early. I noticed how hard Luca and Nicu tried to hide their disillusionment. But somehow, I felt at peace with my decision. I sensed something around the corner waiting for me.

Three weeks after I came back from Germany, Luca told me of a youth convention in Braşov, three hundred kilometres from our church. I thought it would be a great opportunity for me to get to know the other young guys from church as we would share the same house during the conference.

Once at the convention, we settled into the house. I admired Luca for his dedication to us. Behaving like an older brother, he loved answering the innumerable questions we had before bedtime. One night we stayed up till 3 AM listening to his story about how he got to know his wife and his adventures in the Netherlands studying theology. I could only imagine the millions of bikes and the windmills. Like a beacon on a faraway cliff, Luca awakened an outlandish desire to go and visit the country one day.

On the last day of the conference, Luca introduced me to Manfred, a tall German-looking man.

"Nice to meet you, Alex. I am the director of a Bible college in Sibiu," said Manfred in perfectly articulated Romanian, shaking my hand with a confident squeeze.

"Likewise," I said joyously. "What exactly does the college teach?"

"Our vision is to equip new believers with the biblical knowledge they need to be able to navigate the surge of questions they are confronted with, once they've embraced the Christian faith."

"Is it meant for those who have been going to church for a while, but who're still struggling to understand certain theological issues?" I asked.

"Yes, absolutely. Are *you* thinking of enrolling?"

"Well, I have to admit that it feels like an answer to a prayer. I will think about it. Thank you very much. I will be in touch."

• • •

I could not concentrate on the conference's program anymore. The idea to set aside two years of my life, to study the Bible together with other men guided by Manfred's wealth of knowledge captured my mind.

My imagination buzzed, devising plans. I'd never been to Sibiu, but I'd heard many stories about its famous *Podul Minciunilor*, The Bridge of Lies. Legends say that on this bridge, thousands of couples vowed eternal love to each other. The story became famous in 2007, when Sibiu was elected as the cultural capital of Europe. I couldn't wait to visit the Brukenthal Museum one day, to see the paintings of my favourite painter – Peter Paul Rubens.

After I came back from the conference, I entertained the thought of telling Luca that I was interested in enrolling at the Bible school. For the next two weeks, I prayed and contemplated how my future would look in Western Romania.

"Have you thought about whether you would like to go to Sibiu?" asked Luca after the service one Sunday.

"I did. I'd absolutely love to, but I cannot possibly afford it," I declared.

"I had a conversation yesterday with the church council and we decided that if you chose to study in Schellenberg, the church would support you financially," said Luca, smiling.

"I don't know what to say … I am beyond ecstatic!" I replied radiating happiness.

"We believe that's what you need to do and we'd love to be part of your journey."

*   *   *

I felt deeply affirmed and loved by my new family. In the weeks leading up to the enrolment deadline, I realised that my future was tied up with the Bible school. I was so excited about the thought of living together with other people who loved God and who were interested in deepening their knowledge of the Bible. The longing to discover who I was felt intrinsically connected to that school.

On my last day in Cislău, I wrote a poem called *Euphony*, inspired by Psalm 122 and thinking about the wonderful two years I envisioned I'd have in Sibiu:

"I smell the fragrant oil abundantly poured
When my sisters and brothers are saying:
'Let us visit the house of our Lord!'
I long for the singing and desire the praying
Brought in the presence of our affectionate God.

Peace glues our hearts together in a brotherly cluster
While gratitude is lifted on wings of orisons.
We seek Your presence and its enthralling lustre
Breaking our pride and our earthly horizons.
We embrace Your peace, Your goodness and love."

• • •

Luca offered to drive me to the boarding school. On the road we talked convivially, his engaging personality made me feel heard, as I immersed in self-exploration and betterment.

As he pulled into the driveway of the school, I was dazzled by the sheer scale of the place and its architectural features. On each side of the road, houses were set in rows of up to fifty. Unlike the villages in southern Romania where houses were set back from the street and the front garden, the houses in Schellenberg were directly on the pavement. Tall and colourful, the walls facing the roadway acted like a shield, protecting the privacy of each household. To reach the front door, one had to drive through a tunnel, built into the house. It felt like time had stood still since the late mediaeval era.

Having driven under the dark orange building which shielded the school from the bustling main street, we then headed into another building, until we reached a vast courtyard. A grand lush lawn bordered by shamrock green conifer trees was divided by a paved alleyway that led to the school building.

The building was floral white on the upper half, and russet brown on the bottom half. Insulated from the village noise, the courtyard stood serene, and imbued with an early autumn smell. Being Friday evening, the only other person in the building was the housekeeper, a woman who despite her short stature, exuded confidence and energy.

After climbing two flights of stairs, we reached a lengthy marble-floored corridor with doors on either side. Opposite a generous-sized sitting area, she showed me to the room where I'd sleep for the next two years. As I entered, I could see a single bed with a metal frame and a shelf above, holding a couple of aged books. Next to the bed was a small shower cubicle lit only by a lightbulb. On the far corner from the door were two other beds and a large wardrobe. I chose the bed nearest the shower because from there, I could see uninterrupted views of farmland through the window.

Before leaving, Luca helped me with my luggage.

"Well, my mission is now over," said Luca, with his usual cheeky smile. "Yours is about to begin."

"I am so excited, Luca. I don't think I have ever been like this."

"Positive, I hope," he added.

"Oh yes … very. You have no idea how grateful I am for your

help, and for what the church is willing to do for me," I said giving Luca a hug.

"I am a phone call away, if you need me. And *He* is even closer," he replied, pointing towards the sky, grinning.

As he got into the car, I realised I'd be on my own in this new world. His eyes smiled through the dirty windscreen; I waved holding back tears.

• • •

Back in my new room, I sat on the bed taking in what had happened in the last 40 minutes. The housekeeper had left after giving me instructions on how to lock the front gate in case I wanted to explore the surrounding area.

For the first time in my life, I slept on my own in a building devoid of any other human being. I was afraid of the dark, but I told myself that a nineteen-year-old needs to rationalise those fears. I could see the stars through the window as I was praying.

Suddenly, a strange memory filled my thoughts. I realised that years before, I had woken up from a dream that had a pre-scient aura about it. The alien room that I'd seen in that dream and that kept me awake, was the same room in which I was now, at the Bible school. Could it be God's way of confirming that I had arrived where I was supposed to be, according to His foreknowledge?

• • •

After the weekend, the other students arrived one-by-one, each choosing their place to stay for the duration. A thirty-some-thing-year-old man was the first to choose the same room as me. After exchanging a couple of sentences, I was sure we'd get along very well. The other guy that chose our room, I'd heard something of in passing, after a church service in Nehoiu – I knew he'd come to the Bible school but as he went to another church, we hadn't really talked.

We shared the toilets with half-a-dozen men and the shower with the other guys in the room. I enjoyed this arrangement very much as it gave me the impression that I lived in a big family. Sometimes, I did crave my own space, so I'd seek out some isolated part of the building, where I'd spend hours listening to music, or reading my Bible.

· · ·

Mathilde was the first close friend I made at the school. What first attracted me to her was her accent, and the foreign way she spoke Romanian. Her Germanic outward appearance looked very exotic to me. This beautiful young woman had a confidence and feminine liveliness I'd never seen before. When she told me she came from Switzerland, I knew we'd hit it off.

Using the pretext that I could teach her Romanian, while I improved my English, I'd use every opportunity to be in Mathilde's company. Perhaps considering her like the sister I'd never had, her being felt familiar, comforting. She said that my artistic personality and chaotic energy reminded her of her brother, who was also an artist. She inspired me to start writing poems again, as I allowed God's light and grace to illuminate the darkest areas of my heart.

The absence of dissention and conflict in my new home helped me become a calmer person. I'd no longer become bad-tempered when someone made me feel uncomfortable. My prayer times with God increased in length and depth, though

I still found it incredibly difficult to envisage Him as a father without attributing characteristics of my biological dad.

Because Mathilde had been a Christian much longer than me, I went to her every time I had a theological question. She patiently and prayerfully expounded the Scriptures to me, allowing me to see the connections between Bible verses and theological concepts.

Manfred's family warmed up to me very quickly. He and his wife had three daughters and two sons. I loved playing with the boys, and they quickly saw me as part of their family. Numerous Sunday lunches would be spent at their place after church, entertaining the boys before their afternoon naps. I admired Manfred's family for the way they loved each other and served the Lord. As I washed the dishes after we had lunch, I'd so often contemplate how my life would've been if I'd been born in a family like theirs.

Six months into my education at the Bible school, I noticed I was being affected by the creation of secret romantic relationships within our cohort. Seeing them holding hands around the corners, when no one was watching, made me incredibly jealous. A wave of depression swept across my mind like a gale. The loneliness and the desire to be comforted led me to seek solace in masturbation and pornography.

Some days I barely ate anything, flooded by an ocean of guilt because of the internet searches and the thoughts in my head. I'd discovered an online forum that allowed me to communicate with gay people from all over the world. The special feature of this program was that with every text message, I could attach a picture that the computer took once I sent it. It became the sole source of comfort and attention.

Communicating with so many people on the forum and

getting to know their *coming out* stories, became the catalyst for desiring to talk to someone about my sexuality. Chatting to men online, only confirmed to me that I was gay, and the men I chatted to encouraged me to talk with my friends about the turmoil inside me. On the app I had created another *persona*, devoid of any religious identity, because of the fear of being rejected for being a Christian.

. . .

I decided to tell Marin my life story. Since arriving in Schellenberg, I had been talking with him almost every day, sometimes for hours. I gave him a short synopsis of the sexual abuse and what changed inside me after that moment. After a deafening silence, he mumbled a few things trying to disguise what I thought was pure disappointment. Our friendship was never the same after that. We still exchanged ideas, titles of unwritten novels and songs, but our hearts never really connected anymore.

I absolutely didn't know what to do with the feeling of rejection I felt from Marin. Mathilde had noticed my reluctance to talk about what was happening inside me, so one day she pushed me just enough so that I gave in.

Leaning with my head against the cold wall of the school's building, numbed by having sat for so long on the concrete step, I began crying as Mathilde held my hand.

"Why can't I just be the way my body tells me to be?" I screamed with all my power.

"And what is it that your body tells you to be, Alex?" asked Mathilde.

"*Poponar*, Mathilde! That is what I am. I am a dumb, good-for-nothing gay guy in a country that hates me."

Mathilde was lost for words. She put her arms around me, and she began rocking me slowly. As I abandoned resistance to her comforting cradle, I cried even more. She just loved me, and that was what I was looking for.

Mathilde continued to talk to me after that day the same way as she had always done. One afternoon, weeks after my confession, she took me for a walk around the village. Her voice had an ominous overtone to it. She began recounting stories from her childhood and the brokenness with which she had to grow up. Through tears she described the trauma from her past that still haunted her.

That day I bonded with her in ways I'd never done with another human being. The shared trauma created an invisible link between our hearts.

"Alex, you need to talk to a specialist about what happened to you because the root of your *problem* is deeply entrenched into your spirit; the abuse made you gay and you need to untangle that!" she said warily.

"I do remember being in love with Maya before Cezar raped me, but I think I felt that attraction towards men since I was a child, Mathilde!" I blurted, confused and a bit defensive.

"It might have been caused by the rejection of your father, Alex!"

"I do remember craving his attention ... and even *his body* ... but I think it was purely for being held by him ... caressed."

"Exactly!" she replied, interrupting the flow of my thoughts. "Your desires were sexualised once Cezar used you."

"I am not entirely sure, Mathilde. It is not what my friends online are telling me."

"I can see why ... never mind ... I suggest you see someone that knows this stuff better than I do."

"I'll think about it. Let's focus on the coming exams first," I said, trying to change the subject.

Mathilde continued investing in our friendship despite what she thought about my sexuality. Her love for me was sincere and full of passion. Like an older sister, she took care of me when I was sick and encouraged me when I felt down.

• • •

My double life online escalated to alarming proportions during the second year at the Bible school. While I was conscientiously serving in church as part of my studies, online I'd have explicitly sexual chats with men from all over the world. After discovering the video chatting capability, I would push the limits even further. The tremendous amount of guilt and shame after such a video conversation absorbed all my emotional energy.

I spoke with Maya on the phone each day, and during one of our daily conversations, I told her that I was sexually attracted to men. "I already knew that, Alex" said Maya with a sigh of relief. Unable to utter another word, I allowed the silence to help me collect my thoughts. When I realised that she continued talking to me despite knowing that I was a *poponar*, my heart was filled with joy and a deep sense of acceptance. That night I loved her more than ever.

The rest of the conversation was focused on an imaginary future when Maya and I would be married and would have three children, somewhere in a distant country where no one from our past would know us. Just before we were about to say goodbye, Maya said reluctantly: "Alex, please talk to your mentor about your porn addiction." After I uttered an unconvincing "yes" and hung up the phone, I admitted that she was right.

* * *

Her suggestion haunted me for weeks until I decided to talk to an elder at the church affiliated with our Bible school in Schellenberg about my struggles. He invited me to his house for more privacy. After climbing a steep and narrow set of stairs, I was invited to sit down on a comfortable sofa in the attic, which he converted into a lounge room.

"So, Alex, let me hear what is bothering you!" he said in a comforting voice.

"I cannot stop the compulsion to masturbate ... I use porn to help me focus ... I am never comfortable imagining the fantasies. I don't know why."

"How did it start?" he asked.

"It started as a way to make me feel better. I have been quite upset that I am not in a relationship like all the others," I answered ashamed.

"You mean, at the Bible school?"

"Yes!"

"Okay. Well, that is another discussion! What do you feel when it happens? What are your emotions telling you about the turmoil happening in your heart?"

"I feel jealous ... and alone. I guess doing *it* helps me be happy again," I added, feeling the blood colouring my cheeks.

"Okay. Those are the things we should first work on."

This was the first time I'd confessed my secret life to a pastor, skilfully leaving out the part about me being a *poponar*. He seemed interested in my story and genuinely offered to walk alongside me. I felt encouraged by his warmth and the Bible verse he gave me on a piece of paper: *So if the Son sets you free, you will be free indeed – John 8:36.* I believed it. On my way back to the school, I sensed a huge weight lifting from my shoulders. I was no longer alone in my struggle.

Meditating on Psalm 25, back in my room, I found inspiration to write *Irenic Plea*:

My soul's eyes are directed towards Your Throne –
Embellished with trust in Your unending forbearance.
Let me not be ashamed under the cold gravestone
Let my enemies not prosper in their hate and
abhorrence.

Teach me Your ways, the path to Your truth –
For there resides salvation.
Disremember the sins committed during my youth –
They have caused me isolation and damnation.

My Lord! You are good, gracious, upright.
Pull me out of my undying distress.
Consider my affliction and this life-threatening plight
And guard me against those who transgress.

• • •

My mother's birthday was coming up in a couple of days and I couldn't ignore a voice urging me to call her and tell her that I loved her. I knew that no one had probably told her that in her entire life, not even my father.

In my prayers, I'd been telling God that I'd like to forgive my mother for everything she'd done, but that I wouldn't be able to tell her *te iubesc*, those two Romanian words no one had ever said to me.

"Hi, Mum! *La mulți ani* [Happy birthday to you]!" my voice shook.

"It is good to hear from you, Alex. Thank you very much. You're the first one to congratulate me.

Hesitantly I said: "*Mama*, I wanted you to know that I am happy that you are my mother. Regardless of the history between us, I am grateful for the fact that you took care of me. I am genuinely proud of you and *te iubesc*!"

Those frightful last two words were said in such a hurry, like when one's bus comes earlier, and the goodbyes need to be said sooner than expected. I could hear sobs at the end of the line just before she hung up.

Was that too much for her to hear? I decided to wait and not redial. After ten minutes, my phone started ringing.

"Alex," Mum said in between the sobbing, "I never expected you to ever say those words to me. I am still shocked. My body is shaking like the '77 earthquake. Why now?"

"Recently, I discovered that God loves me more than I can begin to imagine … He forgave all the nasty things I've done … to you, to Adi … even to Dad. God taught me that the grace I've received from Him, I have to pay it forward to those that have wronged me. Don't think that this was easy … I fought with Him for the past days like with a lion, but I knew I had to forgive you …"

"Have you … forgiven me?" asked Mum crying.

"I think I did … I do … I do forgive you," now both of us were crying.

"Thank you, Alex. I feel like a flower that has finally bloomed, feeling sunlight for the first time in my life."

"You aren't the only one, I feel lighter as well. If minutes ago I said that I love you, now I feel *it* as well."

"Can I call you later? I still need some time to let it all sink in. I am unravelling," said Mum before hanging up for the second time. I felt like I had just talked to a totally different mother.

• • •

After that day, something in mum began to shift. Like a dove being released from a life-long cage, Mum began to feel emotions besides anger and fear. The phone conversations with her started to be marked by happiness, hope and a peculiar sense of reconciliation. Months after her birthday, she sent me a long text message:

> My dearest Alex,
> I want to ask for forgiveness for the way I treated you growing up.
> Firstly, I want to say that I did not mean those words years ago wishing you were never born. I simply did not know how to control those feelings inside me. I was out of control Alex. I still am.
> I apologise for the harsh punishments I inflicted on you. I cannot even recognise myself in the person I was then. I saw the anger and hate in your eyes and that made me beat you even more. I am sorry.
> What I am about to tell you is not an excuse; I just want you to know that I also bear a heavy load on my heart. Your grandmother tried to kill me when I was a little girl, and she hated me all her life. I don't think I knew how to be a mother myself. I mean, how could I?

I hope you can understand. I chose to write these things because I was afraid I could never tell them face-to-face. This is my way of saying that I want us to start again. I want to be a better mother.

Alex, your God must truly exist, because without a divine power you couldn't have forgiven me on your own! I hope I can get to know Him as well.

Te iubesc,

Mama

I began crying uncontrollably. Those two words … I had desired to hear them from Mum all my life. Now that I had, it almost felt too good to be real. I felt as if the world around me was spinning like a disco ball reflecting episodes from my past onto the walls of the room. As each episode came out, its impact on me vanished. I felt an instant release from the hate, the anger, and the hurt that had built up in me from those events.

I was elated to know that my mother noticed a transformation in my character and that she was able to see God working in my life, despite the way I felt about myself. I wanted to start again, feeling the excitement rising up. I was so grateful to God for extending His love for me to Mum. On the bed, the Bible was open at Psalm 21. After I read it, I began writing *Panegyric*:

My heart welters in the waters of Your words
it blissfully swims
and cheerfully beats
slowly advancing towards
the inlet where You're waiting for me.

My life is coloured with the splendour of Your blessing
it peacefully lives
under terrestrial horizons
enrobed in gilded caressing.
Thank You for Your softening soothing.

A week after her emotional text message, Mum called to tell me that she was thinking of reading the Bible. One morning, as I was studying for an exam on the Old Testament, I received a text message from her saying that she had just finished reading Genesis. My heart sung of joy knowing that Mum decided to seek the God whom I'd dedicated my life to.

. . .

At the end of the first year at the Bible school, I went to Cislău for a couple of weeks, so that I could talk to Mum about her journey reading the Bible. She seemed lighter and her face had an aura that I hadn't seen before. I also noticed that she swore much less, and her bursts of anger were less effervescent.

Adi looked more mature; his voice had grown deeper and he was taller as well. I could feel his affection for me in the hasty but strong embrace he gave me as I entered the living room. We'd been drifting apart because of the distance but I still loved him more than anybody in the world.

Mum was reserved in showing much affection but inside her eyes, I saw a flicker of joy I'd never seen before. My father shook my hand with his familiarly strong grip and gave me a fleeting peck on my left cheek. This new routine of greeting my family, after being away for long, flooded my heart with warmth.

. . .

I'd missed my mother's cooking, maybe just as much as my secret place under the willow tree on the riverbank. I'd spend almost every day of the summer writing poems under its shade as I'd listen to the river's whisper. Early in the morning, I loved taking a stroll along the river as I prayed and meditated upon numerous theological concepts.

My mother sold sea buckthorns to people from all over Romania, and some days I'd go with Adi to the meadows around the village in search of the orange shrub that produced the sour berries rich in vitamin C. One afternoon, as we'd exhausted the typical conversational topics, like cars and video games, I felt compelled to ask my brother about his faith. I knew that when he had been a young teenager, he loved to join me going to the Orthodox church in the village. He never really spoke of religion or faith, but I knew that he meditated on the things he'd heard in church.

"What did you think when you heard I got baptised in the Brethren church?" I asked.

"I was very happy for you. I knew that was what you really wanted. But I was dreading Dad's reaction. We both know what he said," replied Adi, with a wide smile revealing a mouthful of yellowed teeth. *Is he taking care of himself?*

"Yes. I didn't expect an embrace and a *I am so happy for you.* You were there when he said that he'll never love me. So, no expectations there," I said half-laughing, half-crying.

"I'd like to know more about your faith, Alex."

"You do?"

Unable to contain my happiness, I shouted "Hallelujah", echoed by the forest around the meadow. When I asked Adi whether he'd like me to tell him more about my faith that afternoon, he said with a big smile, "I can't wait!"

When we arrived home, I showed him Bible verses that spoke of the gospel and life as a Christian. He stopped for a few minutes at Luke 15:6, "Rejoice with me, for I have found my sheep that was lost," and began crying.

As I put my arm around his shoulder, he looked deep into my eyes, and said sobbingly: "I am that lost sheep!" My tears flowed like a summer rain. I felt instantly connected to my brother, in a way that was almost magical. I prayed with him, helping him formulate in words his inner thoughts to God.

My love for him increased to heights never reached before. He radiated happiness, the way the sun reflected its warmth and brilliance in the Buzău river. For the first time in a decade, we went fishing together. We had to descend through a dip to reach the river. The wild flowers embalmed the atmosphere with a sweet aroma, as the tamed warmth of the July sun caressed our bodies full of excitement.

"What happened to Mum?" asked Adi.

"What do you mean?"

"She is so unlike her ... sometimes it looks like a totally different person," continued Adi.

"We had a conversation a couple of weeks ago about forgiveness! She told me she *loved* me," I said, enunciating the word under my breath, like something you would hide from the Gestapo.

"I have seen her cry recently. She goes outside in the evening for half-an-hour or so, and when she comes back, I could see she'd been crying."

"I truly believe that something in her is changing. Just like in your heart this afternoon," I declared with a hopeful tone in my voice.

"We have to shut up now ... we are scaring the fish off," Adi replied, clearly wanting to change the subject, probably having had enough of deep conversations for the day.

. . .

My father noticed Adi's sudden interest in the gospel, and then harshly said to him: "If you also dare to convert, like your *jackass* brother, I will kill all of you and kill myself last, as I burn the house to the ground!" Adi's face became ashen. He looked at me for a fraction of a second, and then went outside for the rest of the day.

How could a father say such things to a son? I couldn't stop thinking about my father's words to Adi. I knew that he didn't consider *me* his son anymore, but I couldn't believe he'd kill my brother, whom he loved very much.

As I expected, Adi stopped asking me questions, keeping the interaction between us minimal for the rest of the summer. It took colossal amounts of strength to stop my disappointment towards my father turning into hate.

BECOMING
MY OWN PREY

IN THE FIRST WEEK OF SEPTEMBER, I went back to Schellenberg for my last year of theological studies at the Bible school. The last months of 2011 dragged on, dull, grey, and tedious. I seemed to be unaffected by the new subjects, nothing particularly spiked my interest. The experience with my father awakened the dark monster inside me, feeding on the attention I'd get from other men. I doubled life on the internet, hanging onto every compliment.

One day in the beginning of January 2012, I looked on the web for people in Sibiu, the city near Schellenberg, who might also be *poponari*. Jumping from one webpage to another, I stumbled across a private event happening in a week's time, in a private home, welcoming gay and lesbian people from the area. My heart beat faster than the pendulum of the cuckoo clock on the wall. I knew I'd be a fool trying to resist the urge; in the end I would go.

The night of the event came around in the blink of an eye. I left the dorm without telling anybody where I was going, not even to Mathilde. The excitement of doing something so covert and furtive, with the teeming rivers of adrenaline in my veins, helped me disengage the thoughts that would've otherwise stopped me.

. . .

A twenty-something year old guy opened the ornate wooden door, shaking my hand and greeting me with a genuinely welcoming smile. As I followed him through a corridor illuminated with a diffused light, I could feel the vibration of the bass coming off the walls.

We reached the basement, where I was welcomed by a handful of men and women of different ages. The guys danced slowly to mellow tunes, wearing colourful partially unbuttoned shirts and tight trousers. A couple of girls cuddled each other on a green velvet couch at the back of the room, giggling and talking animatedly. Shyly, I took a seat on one of the chairs near a three-seater couch, drinking in the atmosphere.

A surge of anxiety flooded my mind. The fear of being recognised paralysed me. Trying to shake off the thoughts, I realised that someone was talking to me. Touching my hand, a young man with curly hair and dark brown eyes smiled awkwardly, asking me whether I was alright. Like a bolt of lightning, I jumped up and headed for the front door, excusing myself apologetically.

The shock of the cold winter air hit me as if I'd just walked through a plate-glass window. I couldn't believe that I'd been so foolish as to give into my desires to meet these people. The charged atmosphere and the sensuality of the place stuck in my mind, like a fly trapped in a spider's web unable to move. Something inside me shifted.

I didn't feel I could tell anybody about what I'd just done. No one could possibly understand the mountainous intensity of my desire to be loved and embraced by a man.

• • •

Before I knew it, I was again surfing the internet for gay men in my neighbourhood. One night, around midnight, I found myself in a dilapidated neighbourhood of Sibiu, meeting a man I'd briefly chatted with online.

He'd mentioned that he'd like some company to share a bottle of Shiraz. Consumed with the longing to be in the presence of a man who understood what I was going through, I decided that I would join him.

He came to the station where the bus had dropped me off, and I followed him as we walked together to his house. As we reached his front door, an ominous shiver ran up my spine. The dim light coming from a small table lamp bounced off the low ceiling. The smell of mould and old coffee grounds ramped up my discomfort.

He invited me to sit down on a well-worn couch covered by a flowery carpet. As he positioned himself next to me, I could smell his breath tainted by cigarette smoke. Trying to hold my breath and stop my body from shaking, I stood up and decided to admire his movie collection, in a vintage cabinet. He joined me, embracing me from behind. As I sensed the warmth of his body through my clothes, and his lips touching my neck, I screamed inside. Unable to concentrate on small talk, I grabbed my coat and left the house. Running towards the bus station, I heard him calling my name; I jumped into a taxi.

My body shook so hard I could barely tell the taxi driver where I wanted to go. I knew that night could have ended disastrously. My lust and longing to be loved by a male, emotionally and physically, had brought me into dangerous settings.

I'd promised myself and God on that drive back to the school, that I wouldn't be seeking out men in Sibiu anymore. I could risk being expelled from the Bible school and ostracised by everyone I knew in Sibiu.

Life continued as normal after that night, including my online double-life. Mathilde didn't suspect a thing, and I couldn't muster the courage to tell her.

* * *

For the duration of my studies at the Bible school, I prayed every day for my attraction to men to be taken away from me; I would tearfully implore for hours at the time. Was there something that I needed to do before God would take those feelings away from me? Did I need to be holier?

Drowning in my hopelessness, I found myself talking online with another man from Sibiu. He was studying to become an Orthodox priest at the theological university. I thought that by interacting with him, I'd finally befriend a man who'd fully understand my struggles. I loved his self-confidence and because he seemed interested in meeting me, I decided to give it a go.

That warm summer afternoon, seated on a bench in the central park of Sibiu, I admired the children playing with the water fountain, oblivious to the strangers passing by. I was jealous of their innocence and their blindness to problems and pain.

Fighting back tears, I felt a tap on my shoulder. A surge of admiration pierced my heart as he smiled at me. He was tall, slender, and well-groomed. As I shook his hand, my fingers lingered on his for an extra second, stopped only by the surge of hot blood in my cheeks. Shamefacedly, I invited him to take a seat.

"Have you waited for long?" he asked.

"No, not really. I came a bit sooner because I love admiring the movement of the water droplets," I explained.

"Likewise. It reminds me of home. My parents have a smaller artesian fountain in their garden. When I was a child, I used to bathe in it when they weren't home. Last time I saw it was last year at the end of April, when William and Kate got married. You see, my mum is obsessed with the royal family, and she wanted me to watch the wedding with her. It was one of our little traditions sharing royal events growing up. Why am I telling you all this?" he asked, blushing.

"Oh, I don't mind. I was not allowed to watch much television growing up; and when we did, it was because Mum wanted to watch Spanish soap operas. I learned to speak Spanish fluently, so I guess it helped."

"You see, my father is a lawyer, and my mum is the director of a secondary school in Cluj. They introduced me to the arts when I was in nappies. I learned to read when I was four, and by the time I finished puberty, I had read the complete works of Shakespeare," he added.

I'd never met another man who was so articulate. I hung onto every word he uttered as my mind wandered to a far-away future where our destinies would be united. Shocked by that flash of reverie, I tried to re-engage in our small talk. After a brief awkward silence, he proposed a coffee at his place. I knew he had roommates, so I thought I had nothing to worry about.

Frankincense mixed with the smell of dirty laundry filled the air in his flat. His room was a plain square box featuring two bunk beds with a round wooden table in the middle. Trying not to bump my head on the metal bar of the upper level of the bunk bed, an intense feeling of discomfort and irritation formed in my mind.

Surprisingly I didn't feel any physical attraction to him. My infatuation was solely directed at his intelligence and humour. From time to time, if no one was around, he'd take my hand into his, slowly caressing it with his thumb. If we heard footsteps, we instinctively pulled our hands away.

Out of the blue, he said murmuring: "I want to see you naked, Alex!" My astonishment combined with the words he'd uttered, sent shivers all over my body. Beguiled by his request, I followed him to the bathroom. After he removed his mint green t-shirt, my attention focused solely on his beautifully chiselled hairy torso. Being able to finally touch a man's body without the fear of being ostracised, felt electrifying. Drugged by this alien sensation of sheer bliss, I hadn't realised that we were now both naked, and caressing each other's bodies.

My conscience screamed at me, but the volume of my sensual intoxication was much louder. On the spur of the moment, I pushed him aside. Mechanically putting my clothes back on and without saying a word, I stormed out of the building.

* * *

I couldn't ignore the euphoria I'd felt just moments before. For a couple of minutes, I'd experienced what I'd imagined resembled lovemaking. Though I didn't have any romantic affection for that man, the interlocking of our bodies had electrified my thoughts and emotions to orgasmic levels.

Suspended in my inner reality, dominated by clashing forces, I looked towards the sky raising my fist in rage. Why couldn't

I have what my body was yearning for, without feeling like a fallible human being? *Why did You make me this way, only to not allow me to be with a man?*

Trying to rid my experience with the theology student from my mind, I concentrated on passing my exams at the end of the school year. The arrival of the finishing line reared up like a sudden ravine. As my graduation approached, now only a couple of months away, I began to feel affected by having to move on in another direction in my life.

While surfing profiles on the forum one night, I stumbled across the picture of a smiling Dutch guy posing in front of a beautiful bridge. Intrigued by his handsomeness, I sent a *hi, how are you*, together with a selfie. He replied back within seconds. The conversation continued long into the small hours of the morning, fuelled by the intrigue of getting to know each other.

Kees was in his early forties and had the most amazing blue eyes I'd ever seen, beautifully framed by luscious grey hair. The shape of his face seemed so familiar; it attracted me to him. His carefully structured sentences made the interaction between us so pleasurable. After we switched to chatting on Skype, the conversations became deeper.

A few days after that, Kees told me that he was married to Willem, a guy a year older than him, with whom he'd lived for more than three years. In the months prior, I would've felt distressed at the thought of two men being married, but the recent encounters in Sibiu had opened new avenues for exploration in my mind. Intrigued by his story, I was keen to get to know Kees and Willem better.

• • •

After many Skype conversations, Kees proposed that I come for a short holiday to the Netherlands that summer, stressing that I wouldn't need to worry about the airfare, as they would be more than happy to pay for it. Fighting the temptation to say *yes* immediately, I told him that I'd think about it for a couple of days. I wasn't ungrateful; it just seemed like such a risk. What if they'd end up being like the creepy man from weeks ago? They looked like normal people, trustworthy, and cultivated but I still had doubts.

I'd been living with Manfred's family for a couple of weeks at that time, as the school was closed for two months. I'd decided to stay a few weeks extra in Sibiu before going back to Cislău; I wasn't quite ready to face my parents. I went with Manfred on various trips around Sibiu during that time, mainly because of church planting projects. One afternoon, he told me that it would be good if I could stay in Sibiu and get involved in a program he wanted to kick-start in September that year. I felt incredibly affirmed by his invitation. I could finally see a glimpse of a future after my graduation.

At the end of that week, my doubts had lifted. Instead, a peculiar and rather alien sense of hope floated around in my thoughts, like a Zeppelin suddenly appearing in a twenty-first century city – its presence attracting everybody's attention. I knew that the peace meant I could go to the Netherlands. I sent Kees a message saying that I'd love to visit them for a couple of days.

* * *

July came faster than expected. The flight only took a little over three hours, but it felt like an eternity. If the last time I flew I was excited by the novelty of the experience, now it felt almost familiar, a strange premonition that travelling would become second nature in my life.

Waiting for my luggage in Eindhoven airport, I sensed my knees shaking uncontrollably. My heart raced, and my palms sweated; behind the sliding door, another chapter in life was waiting to be written, and this time I couldn't predict its ending.

As the waiting room came into view, I could see Kees pacing up-and-down and then stopping to wave shyly. His joyous greeting and his funny Dutch accent put me at ease.

"It is so lovely to finally meet you, Alex. *Welkom in Nederland.*"

"Nice to meet you Kees! But wait … On my way here, on the plane, I practiced something especially for this occasion … *Bedankt!*" I grinned proudly, meaning *thank you* in Dutch, the first of many words I'd learn during my stay with them.

"Unfortunately, Willem couldn't come today as he is very busy at work."

"That's alright. Looking forward to seeing him this evening."

"Are you hungry?" asked Kees, as we walked towards the car park.

"I am a bit, but I can wait till we get to your place."

"*Thuis!* It will be your *home* for the next couple of days."

Trying to reproduce the sounds, "*Thaaais, Teeuss* …," I surrendered with a fake grin and said, "I'm sure I'll get the hang of it." In fact, it took me six months to master pronouncing that particular diphthong.

• • •

The journey to Tilburg took thirty minutes by car. My eyes were drawn towards the landscape and the architectural features of the houses I saw from the car window; I struggled to concentrate on the conversation. Kees noticed I was mesmerised by the world passing us by outside. I could see him out of the corner of my eye patiently waiting for my responses.

"Are you alright?" asked Kees.

"Yes! It is so different, it scares me. How can two countries be so dissimilar?"

"I know what you mean. I had the same feeling when I went to America," added Kees.

"What is *uit*?" I said, with a Romanian pronunciation, as we drove past the traffic sign.

"The *ui* sound combination is the same one as with the word *thuis*, that you learnt at the airport," replied Kees, laughing.

"What does it *mean*, though?"

"Oh, it refers to the motorway exit," answered Kees, still sniggering.

We often laughed about this for years to come.

We parked underneath a recently built wheat brown block of flats, surrounded by areas of lush lime green grass. The apartment – decorated in a golden-brown theme – was embalmed in wonderful citrus aromas. After only a couple of minutes of having sat on the couch, I felt at home in their very masculine and composed place.

．．．

When Willem came home in the evening I watched the two of them; I loved the natural way they interacted as a couple. Kees provided direction and vision while Willem added depth, introspection and sensitivity. During their time they spent together they looked like any other married couple in Romania: making food, watching television on the couch in the evening, and housekeeping. I craved to have that level of normalcy with another man.

For the five days we spent together, I felt that I didn't need to be someone else. I sensed this incredible feeling of exploring what my inner self wanted to be. I loved the casual hand on my shoulder when I'd help cutting vegetables for the evening meal, or when my toes would touch Willem's or Kees' whilst watching a television series in the evening.

I began to love them with an intensity that scared me. One evening, the doorbell rang. Kees' parents, utterly consumed with curiosity to meet the *exotic guy*, came to say hello before I went back to Romania, the following day. Kees' mother was absolutely beautiful, and refined. Her husband seemed like a humorous man, stylishly exuding a sense of self-confidence that seemed charming to me.

Having Kees' parents over for dinner I felt part of a lovely family. As they left to go back home, we stood outside of the front door, frantically waving at them pulling out of the driveway, saying *Houdoe!* – the southern way to say goodbye in Dutch.

For the next four days, it looked as if I was living in a fairy tale. We visited breathtaking places in the area. I couldn't understand what people were saying, and that helped me to concentrate on taking in every detail. *Where has this been my entire life? Thank you, Father, for giving me the chance to experience this beauty.*

* * *

My flight back to Romania was one of the saddest moments I'd experienced in my twenty-one years. Pretending to look at the woolly off-white clouds through the small oval aeroplane window, I let a couple of tears fall down my cheeks, only to swipe them off with a swift hand motion. My heart was pulled like a magnet back to the green rainy landscapes, populated by incredibly tall people, who spoke one of the strangest languages in the world.

On the way to Cislău, the world outside the train window looked tasteless and acrid. It smelled of the past, regress, and dreams burned at the stake for the sake of conformity. I already missed the warm embrace of the Netherlands – a harbinger of a multi-coloured future in which I could be whom I wanted.

As I hugged my mother, just having arrived from the airport in Bucharest, she caught sight, for a brief second, of the new man growing inside me. She knew that I wouldn't be living near her anymore. The two years in which she'd seen me only twice, would be a foretaste of a lifetime with her son living in another country.

Her gaze was different, unnerving. The kiss she gave me on both cheeks was more than just a peck, it was loaded with affection and meaning. I put my arm around her shoulder and walked towards the house.

I was overjoyed seeing my brother again and feeling his earnest embrace. His facial hair had grown, and his voice sounded rather manly. My father shook my hand in his usual fashion and kissed my left cheek, hastily. I must've subconsciously imprinted a sturdy dose of self-confidence in the handshake, because he retracted his hand briskly.

Being back in Cislău felt so unnatural and distressing. I was a different person to the one who left home two years before. I could no longer live in an environment dominated by archaic ideas and concepts. My old life was slowly fading away as I was becoming a man.

• • •

In the weeks after arriving at my parents' I spent countless sleepless nights with restless thoughts draining my energy, like a scorching summer. I couldn't stop thinking about going back to the Netherlands. My conversations with Kees and Willem on the phone always drifted towards me doing my bachelors at University of Tilburg. One day, as I was strolling around the river in Cislău, trying to clear my mind, I felt my phone vibrating in my pocket. It was Kees.

My heart began beating faster, as if I already knew what I was about to hear. "Alex, after a lengthy conversation with Willem, we've decided that if you get accepted to a Dutch university, we will sponsor your studies for the next three years," said Kees in a matter of fact way.

"Are you sure?" I said hesitantly, unable to contain my excitement.

"Yes. We want to be part of your future … to help make your life easier. I think you've suffered enough," Willem answered, coming closer to the microphone.

"I am utterly speechless. Thank you so much. Would you mind if I call you later? I need to allow the news to sink in. It is unbelievable," I added.

"Absolutely! Talk to you later, Alex," said Kees, hanging up.

• • •

When I reached the sacrosanct place under the willow tree, I began crying. Resting my shoulder against its trunk, I prayed: "Father, thank You for giving me the chance to go to the Netherlands again, and this time living there for a longer period. Help me find myself, and bring people onto my path who will genuinely love me. Teach me how to love."

By the time I finished praying, the sun had set, and the stars were twinkling. I could still see their encoded message to me. I had a future. I was welcomed and accepted.

Before leaving for the Netherlands, I wanted to visit my grandparents; it would be a while before I could see them again. Memories from my childhood came flooding back with fragments of laughter, grazed knees, and mischief. My grandfather looked frail, not being able to walk that well anymore. It broke my heart to see him, knowing he used to have such an active lifestyle. Reminiscing about the days when we scoured meadows and hills in search of the lost cows, estranged from the herd, and walking tens of kilometres just to listen to folk music together at the fair, made it impossible to hold back my tears.

Mămaia's teary eyes shone like a million fireflies during a night with the new moon. Her life story etched into her wrinkled face, held secrets that should never be told. Her diminutive stature belied inner strength – the strength to give life and to take it away. Knowing her story diminished my ability to believe in her love for me. Her embrace felt cold and affected.

When it was *Tătaia's* turn to say goodbye, he looked deeply into my eyes and began crying. I'd never seen him cry, and *Mămaia* was as shocked as I was. He didn't utter a word; he didn't have to. I almost heard his voice inside my head saying, "Alex, this is the last time we will be able to communicate with each other. I love you!"

His embrace imprinted itself onto my body like an invisible tattoo, one that to this day, I can still feel. Days after that last visit, his health deteriorated suddenly, not being able to walk on his own anymore and communicate with the outside world in a meaningful way. The only time he'd show any connection to reality was when *Mămaia* talked on the phone with me. When she'd say my name, tears would roll down his cheeks. It broke my heart every time *Mămaia* mentioned that.

Just before I left my parents' place, Mum held my hand for what felt like an eternity. She looked deep into my eyes, allowing our souls to meet in an embrace.

"Thank you for showing me the way, my dear son!"

"Don't make me regret leaving …" I pleaded.

"No. That is your path. You have to go, no matter how much it hurts me."

"I'll miss you terribly, but I'll be back next summer."

"I found you, only to lose you again."

"I am sorry. I would have liked to have more time. But now I have to leave. I love you!"

"I love you, my dear son. May God bless you!"

What just happened? Was that my mother? On my way to the train station, I replayed the scene a thousand times. I felt as if she'd given birth to me a second time. Finally I was her *dear son*.

• • •

On 13 August 2012, I arrived at the airport in Bucharest with my entire existence in a twenty-kilogram suitcase. I was filled with the hope that I'd soon discover who I needed to be, to finally feel at peace with my life.

I was ready to redefine my identity independent of my parents' history and influence. I knew I wasn't going to the Netherlands on my own – I was under God's care, even though I didn't completely understand Him.

As I stepped onto the plane, I took a final look at the view outside, framed by the thin metal door. The next time I'd see this view, it would be another Alex stepping out of the aeroplane. Above the clouds, I wrote *The Refugee*:

I left drops of my dreams on your threshold,
Tears and a handful of memories – untold –
You broke my walls, my facade, my stronghold.
Far away, here and now, I lament – uncontrolled –

Your walls captured my laughs – monochromatic tattoos;
You swallowed my cries like a summer gale.
I hoped to espouse, to cry out, to enthuse
My constellation of days with your tale.

Far away, removed from your womb
Where my ideas were birthed – underhand –
I brought with me your calm, your God, your perfume
To a place I'll call my homeland.

MANUMISSION

KEES AND WILLEM'S SPARE BEDROOM had been previously used as an office. Having space enough for only a single bed, the two-by-four room became the place where I'd only sleep, the rest of the day being spent in the open-plan living room.

I'd never lived in an open-plan style house but I embraced it quickly, especially since I had started to express my inner thoughts through painting, being able to watch television from the dining table – which doubled up as a large horizontal easel covered with a black garbage bag upon which tens of acrylic paint tubes fought for a space around the canvas.

"What you are painting *today?*" asked Kees.

"Well, I want to paint the background teal, if I can actually get the proportions right, and then I'll glue beer bottle caps onto the canvas to form a hexagonal shape …"

"Why hexagonal?" interrupted Kees.

"I'm not sure, to be honest. Anyway … and on top of that, I'd like to glue two big forks and a smaller one in the middle. I'll break some of the prongs. Then, I'll put that string around them."

"What is it meant to symbolise? Us?" asked Kees, perplexed.

"Yes." I said proudly, mixing a rich blue colour into the green base. "I think it's a good concept … broken yet together."

"It is creative," said Kees, betraying his doubt through his arched grey eyebrows.

In fact, when I finished the hybrid painting, I wasn't satisfied with the result – it looked as if it was a primary school project gone wrong. I wanted to object to Willem's wish to mount it on the dining room wall, next to my previous paintings, but I acceded to his wish because in the end I believed in the concept of *Broken, yet Together.*

. . .

One of the first people I interacted with were the guild brothers from the *Royal Guild of Saint Sebastian* that gathered in a café in Tilburg every Tuesday evening. Kees had been the secretary for a couple of years. When they heard that Kees and Willem had paid for my airfare the first time I came to the Netherlands, they decided to reimburse the money, as part of the social project they were involved with every year.

I could hardly even pronounce a word of Dutch, but they tried to talk to me in English. Kees had been the first person in the five-hundred-year history of the guild to have a same-sex partner, followed by a lady who was in a *de facto* relationship with a woman. Their progressive vision, paired with an incredible sense of brotherhood and closeness, made me feel welcome and thoroughly accepted.

I always looked forward to Tuesday evening, at the Boerke, what Kees called the café where the guild gathered. Besides the social aspect of the get-together, the members shot an arrow with a bow at a target at a distance of approximately eighteen metres. Archery was a healthy way to release tension or anger.

The decision to become a member felt natural. Almost like a baptism, Kees and another guild brother stood next to me in front of the members pledging their support in my development within the guild.

I was the first non-Dutch member and non-Catholic to become a guild brother. Pride and humble honour ran through my veins.

"Welcome to the family!" said Kees, with a wide smile.

"Thank you! I feel so loved," I gushed.

"That's because you are, Alex. All these people love you," he added.

Two weeks after my induction, on April thirtieth, the guild went to Lijpark to celebrate the coronation of Willem-Alexander – the first male monarch to reign in over a hundred years. Now that I was a guild brother, I felt especially connected to the event.

Seeing hundreds of people around me with their face painted orange and wearing t-shirts featuring the tricolour flag, I began to contemplate the idea of becoming a Dutch citizen. I'd have to swear allegiance to the new king. *Rather handsome*, I thought, watching him on the elephantine screen at the far end of the park.

• • •

A couple of days after I settled into my new home, in Tilburg, Willem's parents came to meet me. They lived forty-five minutes away by car, in a small village near the province of Zeeland. Being able to talk to them in English gave me a better insight into their lives, without being dependent on someone else's interpretation. They were both warm and kind.

I happily answered the hundred questions – enveloped in

a characteristically Dutch curiosity. They were so impressed with my stories that they decided to go for a ten-day holiday to Romania.

My relationship with Kees and Willem naturally took on a familial overtone. Calling Kees "dad" and Willem "daddy," the dynamics between us gradually changed. They began to refer to me as their *pleegzoon*, foster son, when an acquaintance would ask them who the young guy living with them was.

One morning, getting home at five after having been to a party in the city, I was startled to find Kees sitting on the couch in the dark. Visibly on edge, he simply said:

"What is this, Alex?"

"I have been out with some friends," I replied annoyed.

"I couldn't sleep a minute … I was so concerned for you."

"I appreciate that, I really do, but there is no reason to. I can take care of myself, you know?"

He did not reply; we stood still, in darkness, next to each other on the couch trying to let go of the mutual anger. The raindrops hitting the window pane calmed me. When the anger subsided, I realised that he had been genuinely concerned for me – he was becoming a father.

It took years for me to get used to the idea that I was the foster son of two men, married to each other. Spiritually, I'd been earnestly struggling with the validity of their union, and it made me feel ashamed every time I explained my relationship to them to people in Romania. Most of the time, I'd refer to them as simply friends because of the fear of being rejected and humiliated. Regardless of the immense love I had for them and the amazing feeling when we spent time together, I struggled to fully embrace their marriage.

My faith had less priority in my daily routine the first years of being in the Netherlands. I found a Dutch evangelical church in Tilburg, but I struggled to connect with the members of the congregation. I was used to having deep connections with my friends from the church in Nehoiu, but in Tilburg people felt distant and cold. Besides the language barrier, the conversations would reach only a superficial level. I craved a real and rich fellowship with other Christians.

I went to church less and less, inculpating the apathy of the Dutch, but deep down I knew that my love for God was slowly being quenched. I'd ceased having my devotional session every morning, most often blaming the demanding studies which required a significant amount of time every day.

• • •

The reality of soon starting the International Business and Management bachelor course at the Avans University of Applied Sciences in Breda, gave me chills every time I mentioned it. I loved the idea of having to commute the one-and-a-half hours by bus every day, because that would give me time to process that day's events.

The initial excitement wore off rather quickly. The focus on finances and learning how to make more money bored me to death. My classmates were driven and motivated to succeed, while I struggled to even open the books. In November 2012, I noticed that I was displaying the symptoms of culture shock.

Most mornings I didn't want to get out of bed. I only desired sleep, without interruption. Simply hearing something in the Dutch language would make me incredibly irascible, I'd lose my temper, and remove myself. The internal struggle and the battle to allow the new culture's integration within my psyche gave me unbearable headaches. In the afternoon, the pain in my temples was so strong I'd scream into my pillow when no one was around.

I decided to see a local doctor. Based on his referral, a team of medical practitioners took on my case. Together with a physiotherapist, we tried different body postures that encouraged relaxation and destressing, hoping that it would produce some changes. After my eyes had been checked, the ophthalmologist prescribed some corrective glasses. The MRI at TweeSteden Hospital in Tilburg proved that there was no tumour in my brain. The neurologist prescribed me pills to take for the next three months.

The medicines made me feel detached. Most days I couldn't remember what I'd done the day before. I continued going to university, but my interest plummeted even further. Not being able to fully concentrate in class, I had to retake most of the exams in the first semester.

• • •

Being in the Netherlands, I discovered apps that used the GPS to show me gay men in my area and beyond. Within days of installing one, I received a message from Xander, who turned out to be an old colleague of Willem's. Flattered by his compliments to me, I decided to respond to his invitation to have a drink.

I'd always considered older hairy men my type, but Xander was smooth and only eight years older than me. Despite his age and lack of hair, I found him extremely attractive; tall and of chubby build, this made him rather masculine and brawny.

He picked me up from home, and we drove to a town called Heusden, a thirty-minute journey by car. I was so comfortable in his presence, without feeling the need to pretend to be someone I wasn't. Directing my gaze at him from time to time, I'd quickly smile, transfixed by his good looks and charm.

Heusden was magical. Started as a settlement on the river Maas, the city became a fortification in the thirteenth century, surrounded by water. The architecture of the houses reminded me a little of Schellenberg. For the first time in months, I felt my heart beating with joy again. Reaching the fortified centre of the town, I couldn't believe how beautiful and quaint that place was. As I sat on the terrace, waiting for Xander to come back from ordering our drinks, I briefly looked towards the sky, and I whispered a quick "Thank you, Lord!"

I couldn't take my eyes off the huge charcoal windmill with white blades, demanding my attention. Its hypnotising revolution, synchronised with the slow tide of the water from the harbour, captivated my thoughts. I hadn't realised that Xander had returned, quietly studying me as I was lured in my own Ulyssean odyssey.

He gently touched my hand, sending electric needles all over my body. His smile made my mind sing. My culture shock and the headache faded in the background like the sound of a faraway aeroplane in the sky.

"What are you thinking?" asked Xander.

"I'm not sure I am *thinking*, I am just enjoying this moment. Too bad the sun has gone again," I added, looking at the dark grey clouds.

"Welcome to the Netherlands!" said Xander laughing.

"This place has just become my favourite, *ever*!"

"I'll take you to other places, if you want!"

"Is there anything lovelier than this?" I asked.

"I will take you to Vaals next time. You won't want to leave."

"I like your confidence. And not just now … you have this sense of self-assurance that is very attractive to me."

"Aww … thank you, Alex. Maybe after you get to know me a bit better, you'll discover that it's all a façade," said Xander, smiling again.

I was taken aback by his remark. "I'm sure that's not true … I am seldom wrong."

We looked up as the first drops of rain drew damp polka dots on our shirts. "Let's get you home to your *daddies* before we get soaked," said Xander standing up.

On the way back to Tilburg, I put my hand on his right leg hoping that he'd hold it in his hand. When he did, feelings were released like captive horses set free. I couldn't understand why I already felt that I loved him, but I didn't want to rationalise it.

• • •

The next two months, we'd see each other every week. One weekend at the end of November, I decided to sleep over at his place. When we entered his house, he embraced me tightly, and after he gave me a mellow kiss, he said soulfully: "Alex, I think you are an extraordinary young man. I love you with all my strength!"

I felt my breathing stop for a couple of seconds, unable to process what I'd just heard. As he wiped my tears away, I blurted sobbingly "I love you, too, Xander!" We collapsed on the couch, abandoning myself into his embrace, with my head on his chest, soothed by the sound of his heartbeat.

We watched *Dredd* that night, cuddled into each other on the couch.

"I'm so happy you're here, Alex!"

"For me, this is like a dream. I feel like I'll wake up, realising it wasn't real," I replied, holding his hand tight.

"It isn't a dream. Does this feel like one?" He began tickling me, making us both laugh.

"Let's focus on the movie! We can continue this later."

Waking up next to the man I loved was the fulfilment of one of the greatest dreams in my life. Protected in his arms, I felt happiness like liquid gold flowing through my veins. I had to muffle the sound of my conscience trying to break – with its loud clang – the pink glasses I had over my eyes. I didn't want this feeling of bliss to be taken away from me. The lovemaking from the previous night made me feel at home – I belonged to someone. As I further allowed my emotions to engulf in my love for Xander, the gentle voice of the Spirit ceased to whisper.

* * *

Weeks after first sleeping over at Xander's, I decided to be open to my other classmates about my new boyfriend. Like an ephemeral sense of itchiness in one's body, I disregarded the brief bursts of shame I felt when I mentioned that I was in a relationship with a man. I enjoyed the attention I got from the girls in my class, who thought I was so cosmopolitan and chic for being gay. I had resisted that label all my life, but I didn't care anymore – I was loved by a man.

* * *

One Friday afternoon, Xander took me to Antwerp – a harbour city about fifteen kilometres from the Dutch border – glamorous and rich in culture and heritage. I was fascinated by the myriad of boutiques and cafés. Discovering its beauty together with Xander, made the experience all the more charming.

"What do you like the most about the city, Alex?"

"Even though it's rather small, I love the cosmopolitan vibe," I answered.

"My mother used to bring me here when I was a child and buy chocolate for the winter season. I'd like to go and check whether the boutique still exists."

"Let's go! There are so many diamond shops!" I demanded, amazed.

"Antwerp is the largest diamond district in the world," said Xander, holding the door for me as we entered a small boutique. The smell of chocolate hypnotised my senses – I *needed* to touch, to smell, to taste. "Welcome to little Xander's sanctuary."

"And what a sanctuary, indeed!"

"Shall we have a hot chocolate? I recommend the coconut hot white chocolate," said Xander, grinning like a schoolboy.

When he came back with two bright red mugs, he placed the mug in front of me with a thud, startling me.

"Oh, sorry. Thank you. I was a million miles away. It smells good."

"Look, Alex, we have to talk about something."

Turning my body back towards him, I hid a trace of worry behind a scaffolded smile.

"We might not be able to see each other that often for the next six weeks. I will be extremely busy with the system being implemented." He touched my hand with his fingers, as I was holding the hot mug, looking deep into my eyes. "It will be hard not being able to see you again."

"Work is work, Xander." I held his hand with my free

hand, slowly caressing it. "It will make seeing you again more magical."

"But let's not get all moody *today*. We still have many things to see," said Xander, glancing at the list of places on his phone.

That afternoon spent with him, gave me a glimpse into a future fraught with love and enchantment. As we were crossing the Noordkasteel bridge over the Scheldt, I took his hand into mine and I kissed him hastily, heart bursting with ebullience.

"I love seeing you this happy, Alex! Your face oozes happiness!" said Xander caressing my left cheek.

After the sun had set, we went back to Tilburg. Exhausted from all the beautiful things we had seen in Antwerp, my spirit was still overfilled with joy.

"We'll keep in touch through messaging," he reassured me, hugging me as we said goodbye. "Don't forget I love you."

"I love you too, Xander! Very much …"

• • •

For the following weeks, the contact between us was less frequent, as I was immersed in studies, and Xander's job demanded more attention, as he said in Antwerp. I missed him terribly, especially travelling to university and back. Having *Between Us* by Peter Bradley Adams on repeat, the lyrics "Hey stranger when may I call you my own" haunted me like a predator.

The rainy weather made me even more moody. As I watched rain drops trickle down the wide bus window merging into other rills, the craving for Xander's embraces grew ever stronger.

Having decided to go Utrecht for our next day trip, the atmosphere in the car was uncomfortably different. Xander was quieter than usual and less involved in the conversations.

As we were walking around the Oudekracht canal, fear overcame me. Like in a vision, I could see my own reflection in the water, but not Xander's. Barely moving my lips, I prayed softly: "Lord, is this Your way of telling me that my relationship will end today?"

As I searched Xander's gaze, I could see he was trying to tell me something. Tattooed with pain on the walls of my heart, the words he said next drowned me in a river of desperation and doubt.

"Alex, I feel I don't love you anymore. My emotions have been wiped away, as if they had never been there. I feel you are like a stranger to me now. We can't be in a relationship anymore. I am sorry!"

As he tried to hold my hand, I gently pulled it away, walking in the opposite direction.

"Alex, wait! It has nothing to do with you! It's not the first time this has happened." He caught up with me, grabbed my elbow gently, and made me look into his eyes. "Two years ago, I fell madly in love with a man I met in a bar in The Hague. We were so crazy about each other, I thought we would get married." He broke eye contact, turned, and walked a few steps towards the canal. "After a couple of weeks, my emotions disappeared. I couldn't understand why. And now the same has happened with you."

Briefly looking towards him, with my voice breaking, I said, "Take me back to Tilburg, please!"

Unable to form any thought, I didn't utter a word for the hour-long drive. He gave me a cold and detached hug and drove off, like a vapour in the wind. Almost collapsing, I propped myself up onto the corridor walls leading to the front door of the apartment. I could feel the damp t-shirt touching my chest, wet from my tears. I could hear Willem's parents in the living room, but I couldn't face anyone.

Kees and Willem tried to comfort me for weeks, but I was inconsolable. The life that I had imagined for the past months seemed like a lost pregnancy. The swell of anticipation of so many romantic dinners, and city trips with Xander were reduced to a deafening silence.

Due to his employment, I could only see Kees in the evenings, after he finished work, or at weekends. Willem was home more often thanks to working three days per week, but I never managed to connect with him the same way I did with Kees. One morning, fighting the need to get up, I could hear Willem pacing up and down outside my door.

"Alex, I thought you'd like to join me come to *Tuincentrum* ... you know ... the garden centre we went to last month," suggested Willem, opening the door slightly.

"I'm not sure I'll be very *gezellig* [sociable] today ..." I whispered, covering my head with the duvet.

"I will wait for an hour, before I leave ... I hope you change your mind." His voice all concern.

"Okay, I'll be ready in twenty minutes," I replied, surrendering.

For the next couple of weeks, I looked for solace in the embrace of strangers – men that I'd find on gay apps. Emotionally numb, I'd cling to every deep stare or kiss. How could I get out of that graveyard of emotions when I'd just been rejected by the only man whom I loved with all my strength?

•   •   •

Guy after guy, I felt emptier than ever. No one seemed able to fill the emptiness left by Xander in my thoughts. Along with the messiness of my romantic life, I'd decided to stop my business studies. I was convinced that my calling wasn't to work for a multi-million-euro enterprise.

After three months of careful consideration, I resolved to start a Bachelor of Liberal Arts and Sciences at Tilburg University. Kees was an alumnus, and I knew he would be so proud of me graduating from the same university as him. Every time I'd pass by its vast green campus it pulled me in.

The transition from applied sciences to theoretical concepts proved harder than expected. From the first lecture, I noticed the anti-religion ethos dominating the lectures. My faith and religious beliefs were challenged almost every time I went to class. As I had no other classmate to talk to, doubt began to settle in. I knew I couldn't drop out for the second time, but I couldn't continue either. The attacks on Christianity felt so personal; most days I'd be so consumed with shame for who I was, and what I believed in.

After the first semester, something had to change. After long conversations with Kees and Willem, we decided that Liberal Arts and Sciences wasn't making me happy. For the third time in my life, I was confronted with the question of what I'd like to do with my future. Kees suggested that I study the Dutch language course offered by the university. I wanted to be able to communicate better with the Dutchies, so I decided to give it a go.

* * *

Learning a new language was entertaining. Being fully immersed in the culture, memorising words and phrases seemed an easy task. After only a couple of months of daily practise, I'd become fluent in speaking, and proficient in getting the gist of what was being said.

I then realised that when my foster grandparents were talking about me to Kees and Willem, they were referring to me as *de kleine*, which I already knew was the equivalent of 'the little one' in English. The language was no longer a barrier, I was slowly becoming *one of them*.

Mastering the language brought new opportunities to connect with Tilburgers. On a whim, I decided to join a Christian student association, affiliated with University of Tilburg. I felt I needed to reconnect to Christian fellowship. The news of the Flight MH17 that killed a hundred and ninety-three Dutch people the week before, jump-started my faith.

The people from the student association were incredibly friendly and patient with my botched language. Some of them had lost family members in the tragic event in Ukraine. Being part of the group enabled me to focus my attention on someone else's pain, and forget about my own sorrow.

. . .

I started to consider Kees and Willem's parents as my grandparents. I began to call Kees' dad *Opa*, and his mother *Oma*. Because I didn't want to give the same appellatives to Willem's parents, I called his father *Buni*, and his mother *Buna*. I was overjoyed when I heard them call themselves by the Romanian appellation. Willem's father even used *Buni* as a first name as part of a pseudonym for his poetry. I felt so honoured and accepted as a member of the family.

Spending time with "my Dutch grandparents" became one of the highlights of my week. Almost imperceptibly, *Opa* and *Oma* began to warm up to the idea of having a grandson.

Around October, Kees' family always celebrated *Boertjesdag*, a play-on-words referring to a get-together celebrating the familial bond. Having been invited as "part of the family" and not belonging to the *koudekant* – the ones that had been married into the clan – meant so much to me.

• • •

Kees and Willem bought me a Nikon camera for my birthday, as a surprise. Starting as a hobby by taking random pictures of the family and at events organised by the guild, the reactions of the people who saw my photographs, made me realise that I could do it professionally.

Engaging with the concept of a brand and business identity, awoke the creativity that I thought was no longer within me. My first engagement photoshoot was one of the most exhilarating experiences in my life as an artist. Having the freedom to direct people, to capture an expressive pose, felt so rewarding. Making people smile and immortalising that for them enabled me to begin loving myself. *If I have the ability to make other people happy, then I must have something positive within that brings that out in the people I photograph.*

An American friend, who was on a Christian mission trip to the University of Tilburg campus for a year, invited me to do an engagement photoshoot for her and her fiancé in Berlin, Germany.

My company was going international.

That experience further crystallised the realisation: I was leaving a positive footprint on the world. Excitement at being alive and making people happy gradually grew.

As I walked along the Berlin wall, a mural featuring elderly men kissing caught my attention. The *Fraternal Kiss* by Dmitri

Vrubel awoke my slumberous desire to be with a man. Around me, couples passed by hand-in-hand, giggling and infatuated. Sadness swept over me and Xander's face haunted me; my body ached for him. But I knew I had to bury the memories.

I had to forget. Sometimes I'd find myself daydreaming about how life would have looked had Xander not broken up with me. Would I have done it anyway, when my fragile conscience told me I shouldn't have sex with him?

* * *

After the photoshoot on a rainy Saturday afternoon, I wanted to explore the nightlife of the German capital. Streetlamps and buildings reflected millions of lights like meteors in street puddles. The glimmer reminded me that I wasn't alone.

Suddenly, I was overwhelmed by this gentle sense of peace. Like seeing an old friend after a long time, I felt God's presence engulfing me in an ocean of love. As if a father caressed my face, I felt electrifying tingles all over. People rushed past me, but I didn't want that feeling to end.

Knowing that God still loved me despite of my shortcomings, improved my self-esteem. The next evening, I decided to go to a Hillsong church in the city centre. For the first time in a long time, I felt that I was worshipping God. I knew that His love for me was genuine and His plans would be intrinsically connected to that indubitable care for my life. *I am Yours, Father. Fill me with Your Spirit so I can fulfil Your will.*

* * *

Coming back to Tilburg after a successful business trip to Berlin, Kees encouraged me to participate in a photography competition. The local municipality aimed to promote business opportunities for Spoorzone, a former railyard industrial area set to be revamped.

Strangely, seeing the old locomotives and the dilapidated buildings, memories from the train station in my village flooded my mind. I used to go there as a child with Maya, and dream of leaving my village. I wanted to be far away from the pain and the hate. Little did I know that my wish would be granted many years later.

Waiting for the winners to be announced, I basked in the huge hall – with its grand wired glass panels under a dome – flooded in a silky light. It was like a scene from *Lord of the Rings*, at the coronation of Aragorn.

"Alex, you're shaking," said Willem touching my shoulder. "Are you okay?"

"Yeah …I am just a bit nervous," I answered, trying to look through the mass of people, standing on tiptoes.

Kees came closer to me and put his arm around my shoulder. "It's starting."

To my utter surprise my entry – a macro shot of a railway line, focusing on the curving iron line – was one of the five winning shots. My photograph. The organisers printed them as postcards and distributed them in a welcome package for people who visited the tourist information kiosk in Tilburg.

My heart was so full of joy and pride. As they handed me an official bundle of the five postcards, I fleetingly imagined my parents in the crowd applauding me for this tremendous achievement. I shifted my focus on Kees and Willem's ovations. As I took all the attention in, I sensed self-doubt loosening its grip over my mind.

• • •

After the euphoria wore off, I went back online to chat with gay men again. I craved attention as boredom kicked in. The language course was on a school break, so most of the time I'd spend watching Dutch television, with the pretext of improving my listening skills. In fact, I was just trying to kill time, waiting for men to respond to my chats.

Because I was curious to converse with people from other countries, I sent a message to a guy whose nickname was *sevenoaksbear*. As the name might suggest, he lived in Sevenoaks, a small English town in the county of Kent. After hours of sending text messages, I got to know a lot about him. Terry was thirty-three years old and worked as a salesclerk in a health food store.

His charming wit and dry sense of humour fascinated me. I found myself sending and replying to messages from him all day long. Like a drug, the attention I got from Terry gave me energy and a reason to get up. With an empty agenda and no particular interest in meeting my friends in the city, our online conversations helped me with my ever-present lethargy.

Once we started video chatting, I realised that I was deeply in love with him. Every time I'd see him, my heart beat faster, my body craved his attention even more. When he suggested that I visit him, I simply said, "Yes, Terry. I'd love to."

"Are you really sure he's a safe guy, Alex?" Willem took a seat on the couch next to me and gave me a cup of anise tea.

"From all our interactions *Terry* seems like a really nice guy. Plus, I haven't seen England, yet." I shifted my position, uncomfortable.

Willem arched his eyebrows looking towards Kees who was

working on his laptop at the dining table. "Well, you know that's not a good enough reason, right?"

"Yes, I do. But I might kill two birds with one stone," I stood up, and looked at the lush green grass in the park, through the window.

"What if he's just another Cezar?" blurted Kees from the other side of the room, standing up and coming towards the living room. "What will you do then? You'll be in another country, you won't know anyone …"

"That's not fair," I turned around, facing him, clenching the cushion behind the couch.

"You don't know him, Alex," said Willem, looking at Kees who was visibly annoyed.

"Well, it will be my choice. If I mess up, at least it's *my* mess," I snapped. I caught a reflection of them in the window looking at each other, baffled by my reaction.

I left the room, barricading myself with silence.

*   *   *

After only an hour flight, I was in the train station in Stanstead, looking for Terry. Lost in a sea of hats, parkas, and unknown faces, I could see him coming towards me waving his right hand in slow-motion. He looked a bit different from how I'd seen him on camera. His clothes were worn and of larger fit for the shape and size of his body. Expecting a warm embrace, he simply shook my hand and said, "Hi! Welcome to the United Kingdom!" Story after story, on the one-and-a-half-hour train journey to Sevenoaks I listened to him talking about himself. Utterly exhausted, physically and emotionally, I tuned out for a couple of minutes, only to realise that we were almost at our destination.

We walked to his place on a sloped, wide road, with beautiful oaks lining each side. Just before we reached the gate, Terry stopped and said, "Alex, I live with two other friends. We'll sleep in the same room, on different mattresses. Are you okay with that?"

In my head I was already on my way back to the airport, but somehow, I wanted to give him a chance. *Lord, why is my heart beating so fast?* "Yes, I'm sure it'll be fine," I replied, dragging my suitcase between the rain puddles in Terry's garden.

The front door led to a small untidy ingress. Doing my best not to step onto the muddy multitude of shoes, I followed him into the lounge room, and then into his bedroom. Overwhelmed by the putrid smell of unwashed laundry, dirty plates, and pots randomly dispersed everywhere, I couldn't take my eyes off the old avocado green paint peeling off the walls.

I wanted to leave, but I felt compelled to stay the night. Famished after my journey, I suggested to Terry that we go out and eat something in town. I wanted to escape that place.

I noticed Terry, in the corner of my eye, staring at his feet while we were walking. "Is there something wrong?"

He looked at me briefly. "I know that we said we are only friends, but I feel very attracted to you," he shifted his gaze back to his shoes, both hands in his pocket, fidgeting, "I am sorry."

"That is alright ..." I tried to meet his gaze again. "I'm afraid we have to stick to what we decided ... I only want to be your friend."

A couple of hours ago, on the plane, that would've been a lie, but now after seeing him in person, my emotions had shifted. "Is that alright?"

A grin belied his true feelings, "I'm sure it will be … I can't help if you're so handsome," he whispered, looking around us.

"Thank you, Terry," I said hurriedly, fighting the urge to say 'you too,' knowing that it would be disingenuous. We walked on in awkward silence until we reached the restaurant.

As we walked through the streets that chilly evening, I admired the English architecture glistening in the light cast by the streetlamps. Inside the Italian restaurant, I caught a glimpse of the Terry I remembered from our FaceTime calls. The dim light emphasised his beautiful deep brown eyes.

We talked all night about history, geography and religion. To my surprise, he mentioned that he used to go to a Baptist church when he was younger, but that he'd stopped worshipping when his parents separated. He called himself a *hybrid agnostic*, a combination of traces of Christianity and "a pinch of Eastern religions".

All of a sudden, I was engulfed in an *aha moment*. Perhaps the reason why I felt so attracted to coming to the UK was to help Terry reconnect to my God. As fast as it hit me, my attraction towards him evaporated like morning dew. I was fascinated by his vast knowledge of almost any subject, but my heart no longer skipped a beat.

● ● ●

Back at his place, as I got ready for bed, I noticed that he put the two mattresses next to each other. Trying to think nothing of it, I gave him a kiss on the cheek and moved on my right side, towards the door. After a couple of seconds, I could feel him moving closer, putting his arms around me. Trying to not concentrate on the smell of his sweat, I gently tried to pull his arms away from me.

Flashes of the sty came back to mind. *This is not Cezar, Alex. This is not Cezar.* Like in a slow-motion film, I could see and feel Terry's chubby silhouette shift above me. The reek of his smoker's breath intensified as his lips came closer to mine. Before I could resist, his tongue and lips had already touched my mouth. His weight overpowered my strength.

With his friends being out of town, I knew that no one could hear me scream. When he thrust his mouth into my groin, with all the force I could muster, I pushed him aside and ran towards the living room.

"Who are you calling?" Terry yelled.

"I'm calling a taxi. I want to get out of here," I shouted, my fingers shaking uncontrolled trying to find a taxi on my phone.

Still naked, he came towards me, in the living room. "I thought you wanted it, Alex!"

"No, I did not! You could see and feel that by the way I rejected you. What about our conversation in the street?" My voice increased in volume. "Didn't I make myself clear that I wanted to be FRIENDS?"

"We talked about not letting emotions get involved, but we didn't exclude sex." He took a seat on the couch next to me.

I stood up like lightning. "Oh, please. I didn't mention sex because I thought that you knew what the word *friends* means. And what was *that* about?" I looked towards the bedroom, pointing at the mattress.

"I like it rough … I told you that before in a message."

I was still trying to type in *Google* 'taxi Sevenoaks', but it came out as 'razu Asrbenoaks'.

"Please stay the night, and then you can leave tomorrow morning. You cannot go anywhere at this time."

"Why would I do that?"

"I won't try anything again ... I promise," he muttered leaving me in the living room and closing the bedroom door with a thud.

I decided to stay. Still to this day, I have no idea why.

Even though I moved out of his bedroom to sleep on the couch, I couldn't fall asleep. I packed my bags in the morning, and left. He wanted to give me a hug, as I went through the front gate, but I couldn't allow his body near me. I simply shook his hand, and I went on my way without looking back.

The previous night could've ended so tragically. Why did I put my life in danger, giving into my hormones and my lust? *You will never do this again, no matter how handsome the next guy is!*

*   *   *

Back in the Netherlands, I was grateful for Kees and Willem's support. I didn't sense any judgement coming from their side, only concern for what could've happened.

"We all make mistakes, Alex. I am just so happy that it didn't end worse," said Willem giving me a long hug.

I could sense the care in his voice and embrace. "I thought I was losing my mind that night, Willem. I cursed my darn curiosity a million times ... all night long. Why didn't I listen to you?"

"Sometimes we need to make our own mistakes, in order to learn," he said, masking a furtive smile, rearranging his lampshade moustache.

"That was *deep!*" I added, my voice trembling.

"I mean it." Willem went to the kitchen, taking the kettle from the stove. "We'll always be here for you. *I* will be here for you."

"It feels good to be met with understanding, rather than judgement," I sighed, reaching for his gaze.

"We are not like your parents, Alex. At least we hope we aren't." Willem was now on the couch, opening the package of his weekly catalogues.

"Thank heavens you're not," I replied, joining him on the couch.

My relationship with him grew deeper after my experience in the UK. We'd never been really close even though we knew we loved each other very much. Mainly blaming our different personalities, we knew we'd never become best friends. My escapade with Terry, however, made us talk about profound feelings, which we hadn't previously shared with each other. He told me about his past mistakes, during the first years of exploring his sexuality. It helped me somehow to normalise my tendency to *hunt and conquer* other men for my invisible collection of sexual encounters.

Kees and I had a much deeper friendship. Our favourite spot was on the couch, in the evening, after Willem had gone to sleep – he was adamant that after ten-thirty he should be already in bed. With my head on Kees' chest, we talked about our biggest insecurities, past lovers, or simply about how our day went.

He couldn't understand the complexity of my interaction between my faith and my sexuality. A self-named agnostic, Kees would say to me: "Maybe there is a god somewhere, Alex, but *it* definitely doesn't look like the one your religion portrays." Sometimes, I would throw a Bible verse into the conversation, to steer it into the direction where I could talk about Jesus.

One day, out of the blue, Kees suggested that we read some parts of the Bible together. I had been praying for years for him to be curious about my faith. We then usually selected random passages, reading out loud a paragraph at a time. Sometimes, he asked questions when the text was not straightforward. On Sundays, I noticed that he was listening to a radio station that played contemporary Christian music. I didn't want to ask why the sudden interest, I just continued to pray, hoping that his heart would open even further to the gospel.

On a Sunday morning, as I was preparing to go to church, Kees said that he'd like to join me. *Thank you, Father. I never thought this day would come.* Even though he'd never been to a Baptist church service before, Kees seemed quite involved in the liturgy. Quite dissimilar to the Catholic Mass service, he remarked that the format and the content were rather enjoyable. I was thrilled – my prayer had been answered.

To my surprise, he chose not to come anymore. The reading together of the Bible also stopped, as well as listening to Christian radio stations. I retracted inside my own theatre of thoughts. I was angry at God for not speaking to Kees during church, so that he'd continue coming with me. For the next couple of months, my devotional time was limited to reading a verse or two in the Bible and praying for someone who was sick or in need of emotional support.

* * *

The wounds from the episode with Terry were still open, not yet cauterised. Waking in up in the middle of the night, after an evocative nightmare, I could still feel his sweaty arms around me and his breath in my nostrils. The anger was as raw as that dreadful night.

I knew I was loved by God, but I couldn't feel it lately. I wanted to physically feel safe – wrapped in a man's arms, feeling that masculine energy being transferred into my veins and fill my heart with security. I wanted to feel loved and protected by a man who wouldn't harm me but cherish me, a man who would be willing to die for me. I knew Jesus did all that, but somehow the rational knowledge hadn't translated into emotions – somewhere along the way someone severed that connection.

. . .

My brother and I had drifted apart, but memories of his sweet smile from when we were children lurked in my mind every time I'd see other brothers. He loved seeing me happy. Every so often, I'd wonder what life would've been like if I had him closer to me; together facing the world strengthened by our blood bond.

I felt guilty when I bought an expensive item for myself as I knew he wasn't able to afford it. *Did he hate me now for living such a luxurious lifestyle? Was he envious of the things I enjoyed and the places I'd seen?* Deep down, I was angry at God, for not allowing my brother to have the life I had.

I knew I couldn't trade places, no matter how much I desired it. I didn't know how to connect with him. On the phone, it felt as if I was talking to a stranger, trying to make awkward small talk.

But soon I learnt how to bury those memories and desires in a corner of my being where they wouldn't bother me anymore. I became immune to the flashbacks from my past.

FEEDING
THE SENSES

DURING MY TIME STUDYING the Dutch language course, I spent most of my afternoons in the cafeteria of the university. I took comfort being alone in such a chatty and big crowd. Occasionally, I'd meet a classmate from Liberal Arts and Sciences, but most times I was on my own, trying to concentrate on the online Dutch exercises, eavesdropping on people's conversations. I loved to create scenarios in my head based on what I was hearing.

For a couple of weeks, I had been chatting on one of the gay apps with Chris, a Dutch guy from The Hague. We decided to meet that day in the cafeteria. I'd forgotten the details about him, and I couldn't scroll back because the app would blur chats older than two days, if you weren't a paid member. I knew he was a secondary school teacher, so I could ask heaps of questions about his job.

As I was sipping from my Rooibos tea, I saw a tall figure walk between the sliding doors. I'd met numerous men in the Netherlands who were extremely handsome, but because they were similar height to me or shorter, my attraction would wane after a couple of days.

Chris was different; at least one metre eighty-five tall, had a shaved head – which I didn't know what to think of – and a lovely smile.

"What would you like to drink?" I asked, standing up.

"I'd love a *bottle* of *Spa Rood* [sparkling water], please!" He answered, pronouncing bottle in a British accent.

I smiled and said imitating his accent, "It won't be long, *sir*!"

When I came back from the counter, he was still smirking.

Unaware of time passing, we explored hundreds of topics. With every laugh, his charm conquered a piece of my heart. I was elated to hear that he was also interested in meeting again, but that we'd take our time getting to know each other. As I was still struggling to forgive Terry and begin trusting again, Chris's suggestion was comforting.

• • •

Three weeks later, I invited him to come over for dinner and meet Kees and Willem. He was the second man I'd taken home.

"So, Chris, tell us what do you do?" inquired Kees, handing Chris the roast potatoes.

"I teach religion and spirituality at a secondary school in Zoetermeer," replied Chris putting some roast potatoes on his plate.

"What made you choose *that*?" Kees asked, eyes narrowed.

Chris looked directly into his eyes, widening his nostrils. "I *really* enjoyed learning about different religions, especially in a diverse country like Holland. I believe that children should have a basic level of understanding about those sorts of things.

Kees opened his mouth, about to say something, when

Willem gently shook his head, and said, "That is awesome, Chris. I was raised a Catholic. I had my confirmation when I was eleven, but I didn't continue to go to church after that. I've never really been interested in God. But I can imagine that there are people who are. Right, Alex?"

I coughed. "Yes. That's true. I'd love to be able to teach children the way you do, Chris, one day."

"What are your plans for the future, Chris?" Kees asked, putting his elbows on the table, taking a sip of his wine.

"Oh my goodness, Kees... you are like a detective," I intervened, jabbing the fork into the beef tenderloin.

"Stop being so dramatic, Alex. That's just a normal question. I am curious about his life," rebuked Kees.

"Sorry Chris, we aren't usually this tense," placated Willem.

I could sense the lack of approval in Kees and Willem's behaviour, and stung like a thousand jelly fish. After Chris left, as we sat on the couch, I asked warily, "What did you think about *him*?"

"He was *okay*, I guess ... nothing too special, but nothing too weird either," hissed Kees.

I didn't know how to reply, feeling the top of nose and ears getting warmer. I shifted my gaze towards Willem. "And you?"

"I don't know, Alex. Please don't involve me in this cat-and-mouse game you've got going on with Kees. He was engaging and articulate. That's all I'm gonna say," bellowed Willem, zapping through television channels.

I went to bed that night feeling angry and sad. A part of me detached from my side of our *happy family*. I tried to not take it personally, but I was too addicted to others' opinion of me.

• • •

Our first weekend together was exhilarating. I spent the entire trip on the train to The Hague engaged in an internal monologue between my faith and my desire to consummate my love for Chris. I tried with all my strength to muffle the gentle whisper in my soul. *I need to be embraced this weekend, and having sex with him is the only way I can get that.*

Chris lived on the outskirts of the city, close to the beach in Scheveningen. As we walked hand-in-hand, we left our footprints on the frozen almond sand and I forgot about the world for a couple of hours.

As I admired the reflection of playing dogs and humans on the freshly soaked sand, Chris gave me a gentle kiss, colliding his lips into the skin of my forehead. I smiled and asked him to stand in front of the waves. Being a model, he seemed comfortable with my suggested poses for him. His handmade aubergine sweater a perfect contrast to the dark blue water.

I wanted to capture shots of him, with the tumultuous sea as background. Subconsciously I knew our love wouldn't last, just like the waves that gushed in, but retreated as swiftly and ever-gently as they came.

Watching the sun go down, we sat next to each other on the square rocks along the estuary. As the waves crashed onto the rocks, I playfully squeezed his hands into mine. Like a muted whimper, I hoped others would notice us. I ached for normalcy; fed up with being seen as a freak.

●　●　●

As we walked back to his apartment, Chris talked about his pupils from school. *Could I have my little baby girl whom I imagined I'd call Evangeline, one day? Did I love Chris enough to contemplate a family life with him?* Those inner questions jarred with my spirit, rippling through like emotional hurricanes. I knew I felt comfortable in his presence, and that was enough for me then.

As we cooked dinner, he hugged me and planted kisses on my neck as I cut vegetables for the *Stamppot* – a Dutch dish – potato mash, endive, sauerkraut, sausages and gravy.

We spent the rest of the weekend exploring the city and getting to know each other. This early December, the streets were adorned with lights and artificial snow. I couldn't understand my infatuation for him, as he was smooth as butter and only five years older than me, but I utterly enjoyed the feeling of being in love with him. The night before I went back to Tilburg, I wrote a short poem called *Serendipity*:

> I love hunting your wild dreams.
> Their footsteps pour autumns in my bottomless well.
> Overflowing with joy my eyes beget thousands of streams.
> Our married thoughts skinny-dip in their swell.
>
> I love hunting your evanescent smile.
> Its tree-like lure embraces my lips in a clasp.
> Swimming in a cascade of love my heartbeats lose their rhyme for a while
> Our wedded souls rest their wings in a sacred handclasp.

We couldn't spend Christmas and New Year's Eve together because Chris had made plans with his family before we'd met. I always hated holidays, especially when I had to go to family parties, because I was always unaccompanied. With him on the other side of the country this year was no exception.

Unlike Romanian winter holidays, fraught with arguments

and tears, in the Netherlands I'd been enjoying a delightful time with the family. I wished Chris were there with me, playing games together with *Sinterklaas* [Sint-Nicolaas], or simply holding me in his arms on the couch as we engaged in deep conversations about Christmas.

The New Year's Eve celebration always took place at *Opa* and *Oma's*. Kees' mother loved cooking for the five of us, and some years we'd even be spoiled with a five-course meal. I was enchanted by their love – crystallised after more than fifty years of marriage. Sometimes, when they'd walk ahead of me, I'd admire them like a priceless painting as they'd hold hands. I craved to have someone so committed to being with me, despite my shortcomings and flaws.

As we began to count the seconds to midnight, flashes of 2014 came to mind. It had been a long year – hundreds of frustrating hours spent learning Dutch, the pain in England with Terry, but also having the joy of loving Chris. I knew 2015 would be equally as challenging, as I'd have to think about applying for another university degree. Kees and Willem told me that I'd have to choose wisely, as they couldn't afford another wrong pick. I knew they were right.

After wishing everyone a healthy and prosperous 2015, I went outside to watch the neighbourhood fireworks. *Father, I want to be a better person this coming year. Make Your will known to me, so I can follow Your direction. Help me love the people around me with the strength of Your love.*

As I was praying, I felt the phone vibrating. Chris sent me a text message: "My dearest Alex, I absolutely adored the experience of getting to know you for the past couple of months. I can't wait to create more amazing memories with you! I love you!" As I wiped my tears, Willem waved, indicating we needed to go home.

. . .

I went to sleep rather early that New Year's night. My serene dream about watching the fireworks in Sydney – which I'd seen videos of while I was eating dinner at *Opa* and *Oma's* –took on a different tone. Driving back from the firework show at the Harbour Bridge, the streetlamps switched off, all of a sudden. Blinded by the complete darkness, I began panicking as the brakes wouldn't engage. At hundred-seventy kilometres per hour, with the car not responding to my command, I felt I was going to die.

I noticed a young man standing in the middle of the road. He wouldn't move, no matter my honking and screaming. Fractions of seconds before the impact, I could see the terror of death in his eyes, then a terrible crump as the car hit his body, and it catapulted into the air.

The car swerved to a stop. Breaking the driver's side window, I crawled out of the vehicle through the small opening. A couple of metres away from where the car had come to a stop, the young man groaned in agony. Kneeling down and holding his hand, I realised it was me. As I watched myself dying, a surge of uncontrollable panic took hold. Trying to reanimate the dead body, I woke up.

The darkness of the room made me feel I was still in a dream. I felt my body consumed by fire as I inhaled the fear of dying like oxygen. I must've been screaming because Kees and Willem came running into my bedroom, asking what was going on. "I am dying! I am losing control over my thoughts and my body! I am going crazy like my mother did!"

Voicing the fear of becoming insane as my mother did, growing up in Cislău, made me even more anxious. *What if I am really dying, where am I going to go? I am definitely going to hell! I have to stop sleeping with Chris, that will save me from dying. That's it! I will call him and break up with him.*

Kees and Willem tried to calm me as best they could. As Kees had experienced panic attacks, he helped me concentrate on my breathing. After a couple of minutes, my heartbeat stabilised, as well as my thoughts.

• • •

That morning, I phoned Chris to tell him that because of my mental health, I needed a break from our relationship.

"Is it final, or do you see hope for us in the future?" asked Chris. I could hear his heavy breaths through the speaker.

"I am not sure, love. At the moment it is just too much for me to handle," I lied, haunted by images of the nightmare. I knew that I couldn't be with a *man* anymore, but I couldn't tell him that. I didn't have the energy to explain.

"Then …" He began crying, voice breaking. "…I don't want to hear from you for a while. It will be too painful. I've been where you are; I know how you feel. I love you, Alex."

I began crying as well. "I love you too, Chris. This isn't easy for me."

"I know, love. Get well," said Chris, hanging up before I could say goodbye.

For the next three months, I focused my attention on strategies to help avoid experiencing those outbursts of fear. The dread of turning into my mother terrified me. Spending most early mornings in prayer, I understood that the inner battle between seeking male intimacy through sex and the acknowledgement of its sinful implications, had caught up with me – my mind couldn't process the tension anymore, and so it gave me a warning.

• • •

As Chris decided to take time dealing with his own emotions, I spent my time thinking about what I'd like to study next. In one of the monthly magazines from Evangelische Omroep – a Christian ministry focused on youth and young adults – I noticed an ad for a theological university in Leuven, Belgium. Because the open day would be in a couple of weeks, I had plenty of time to talk to Kees and Willem about doing a bachelor's in theological studies.

The journey by car took approximately one-and-a-half hours. Kees and Willem wanted to join me to get an impression of the place. Full of charm, the towering building had been a Jesuit institute before becoming a university. Surrounded by a beautifully dense forest, I felt I was stepping into a different era.

We participated in two lectures, which gave us an insight into the material that would be covered during the studies, as well as the structure of the curriculum. With some exceptions, the course would be offered entirely in Dutch (most professors, lecturers and students came from the Netherlands). Having finished my Dutch course six months prior, I had the illusory confidence that I'd become even more competent once I engaged with the language on an academic level.

Kees and Willem were adamant that this degree was the right choice for me. I wasn't so convinced, mainly because that would mean not living with them anymore – losing my only source of constant support. The months leading up to my move, I've been praying earnestly, asking for God's guidance regarding my choice of studying in Belgium.

. . .

From the beginning of summer until August of 2015, I'd been working as a mailman for a distribution company in the neighbourhoods a couple of blocks from where I lived. That enabled me to meditate, pray, and prepare myself emotionally for the important move that would take place in a couple of months' time.

The longer I prayed, I realised that studying theology was the right decision. A sense of peace transcended any doubt that entered my thoughts. I increasingly became comfortable with the idea of moving out of my home in Tilburg, after almost three years of having lived with Kees and Willem.

Chris had escaped my thoughts for the duration of my work for the mail distribution company. His absence left a vacuum that was screaming for a refill. I knew I couldn't commit to a relationship with another man. The idea of 'officially' having a boyfriend would send chills down my spine, throwing me into an excruciating episode of small panic attacks.

When the craving for communicating with gay men arose in me, I would enter a trance installing apps, then create a profile, chatting with men, meeting one or two, and feeling self-martyrising shame. Then, I'd delete the profile and uninstall the app. This cycle took place a couple of times a month.

Maybe the most grievous experience after Chris was with Niels, a handsome, tall, hairy, and intelligent Dutch man, in his late thirties. He lived and worked for the Tax Office in The Hague. Having started like a beautiful friendship, once we became more physical, he fell in love with me. In fact, I'd grown fond of him too, but I couldn't admit that to myself. It was too painful.

. . .

During early June, we went to Rheims together; he wanted tour the Moët cellars. Being in France for first time, I fell in love with the Renaissance buildings. Speaking in French – such a romantic language – I reconnected to my amorous side that I'd buried deep inside when I broke up with Chris.

That first evening in the hotel, while Niels was slowly undressing me, I realised I'd fallen in love with him. Despite my body craving the warm masculine embrace, I knew I couldn't deal with another burst of anxiety, so I told him, "I can't be in a relationship at the moment, Niels!" I lied, and it dissolved my inner world like a hole in an aeroplane.

"But why? I thought you wanted *this* as well." He put his shirt back on and opened the door to the balcony and sat on the chair.

I joined him, wiping my tears away with my jumper's sleeve. "I told you how fragile my mental health is at the moment …"

"But why? You seem to change the subject when I ask you about it," he snapped, realising his voice was echoed by the trees of the park below us.

I crouched and put my arm around him. "I am afraid of commitment. I can't do it. Even now, as I speak, I feel the tension rising inside me."

He took his hand and put it on my bare chest where he felt my galloping heartbeat. "I'm not sure I understand what's going on, but I won't force you to feel something that's not there."

I was overflowing with love for him, but I couldn't say a word, the terror had sealed my lips. "I'm sorry, Niels."

• • •

On Sunday evening, our last night in Rheims, Niels took me out for a romantic dinner for my birthday on the rooftop of a glamorous restaurant. My heart raced for the joy of being so loved by a man like him. *Should I disregard my faith and tell him that I love him, and that I can't conceive my future without him? I love him, Father, why can't I be with him?*

He seemed rather unaffected by the conversation of the night before. "So, if you could choose anything in the world as a present for your birthday, what would that be?" he asked, signalling the waiter.

"I haven't really thought about it …" I answered, trying to think.

"I love when you do that," he pointed at my eyes moving from one side to another. The waiter stood in front of us as he was still describing my ritual when deep in thought. Embarrassed Niels said, "*Pourrions-nous avoir un autre verre de Pinot Noir, s'il vous plaît?*"

"I didn't know you could speak French!"

"I am full of surprises. It's not too late to change your mind, you know?" He laughed and held my hand for a second. "I was joking, don't mind me!"

"I deserved that," I said it under my breath, drinking my last sip of wine. "You'll get me drunk with another glass."

"Maybe that is my plan," he laughed, snorting.

"A cruise in Scandinavia …"

"*Pardon?*" He looked fazed.

"My birthday present. I've always wanted to see Oslo and

the fjords. And babies with blonde hair and blue eyes … oh … that language …"

"I cannot give you those," he said, beginning to giggle again. "Okay, I'll stop."

"Are you sure you want *another* glass?" I asked, mimicking the droopy face of a drunk man.

"*Oui, monsieur.*"

We spent the rest of the evening laughing and talking about my unforeseeable future. On the way back to the Netherlands, the next day, I was tempted to disregard my panic attacks, and even my faith, but despite my yearning to be Niels' boyfriend, I decided to let him go. After all, I loved God more. When no one else wanted me, He came looking for me and saved me. Had I not heard that voice, on top of the bridge, I would've been just a distant memory. I couldn't understand why I couldn't live out my love for men in the way my other 'straight' friends did. Despite all my questions and doubts, I decided to trust Him – if not for my precarious mental health.

• • •

The rest of the summer I tried to silence the hollering attractions inside me, like covering up one's face with duct tape. There were moments when I'd wished I'd jumped from the bridge that day. I'd immediately regret thinking that, flagellating myself with the hopes of a *straight* future – whatever that looked like.

I grew impatient waiting for the day I'd move to Leuven. Going to Piushaven – the small harbour of Tilburg – to take pictures seemed to help. Watching the streaming waves crashing into the concrete barriers calmed me, reminding me of my childhood river and the conversations with myself on its banks.

On the harbour no one knew me, it felt as if I was part of the landscape. I'd sit on one of the concrete steps near the water and make up the lives of the people passing by. They all seemed to have a mission, a *raison d'être*. I was still trying to find mine.

With September lurking, I prepared myself for the big move. I was aware of the consequences, but I needed to take my life into my own hands. With little Alex still crying inside for attention, I decided to put my entire existence into luggage once again.

POSTMORTEM

I ARRIVED TWO WEEKS EARLY in Leuven, with plenty of time to acclimatise to the new environment. I was the last person to be enrolled, and only one room was left in the dorm, the smallest one. Only three-by-three metres, the room had a sink, a radiator with a sizeable double-glazed window above and a single bed. That same weekend, Kees and Willem went with me to IKEA to buy a desk, crockery, and cutlery. For the first time in my life, I was allowed to decorate my room with a degree of freedom. There was a dark side to all this freedom that I embraced like a long-lost family member – secludedness.

Solitude scared me, especially when in unfamiliar places. Walking in the Jezuitenpark forest helped connect with the place. The dense foliage of the towering trees looked like hundreds of *kintsugi* pots – slender streams of golden light penetrated the dark canopy. The sound of my steps breaking twigs and bruised leaves echoed between the tree trunks, the forest came to life. Birds chirped, and little animals scampered under dead leaves. Did they welcome or warn me?

The university was only thirty metres from the forest. The cinnamon brown bricks of the exterior walls complemented the greenness of the trees in a wonderful aesthetic symbiosis. There was something mystical about the eminence of the corridors and the scale of the windows. Isolated from the city centre of Leuven, the university offered a great sense of tranquillity – too tranquil for my liking, sometimes.

Once the other students gradually arrived, I began to experience a real sense of community. The *refter*, a big hall adjacent to the kitchen, was the heart of the community and the place where the students came together to eat and debate theological teachings.

Despite having lived in the Netherlands for three years, I realised that my interactions with Dutch people had mainly been limited to those a generation older than me. So I found it difficult to relate to most of the students, because they were my age or younger. Building friendships with the international students helped me navigate that difficulty. We had something so intrinsic in common – our internationality.

● ● ●

Once the lectures started, I became conscious of the difficulty grasping complex theological concepts with a basic level of the Dutch language. I was humbled to find understanding from my lecturers in allowing me to express myself in English, in class and with exams.

For unknown reasons, I had no desire to make connections with my Dutch and Belgian classmates. One cause I suspect is the fact that I'd always perceived them as extremely liberal in their theology. Romanian Evangelicalism had been heavily influenced by Puritan thinking. That meant that when someone became a Christian, they were expected to follow a set of rules. Dutch students, in particular, seemed to have a different outlook on Christian living – they smoked, some drank copious amounts of alcohol, and not a few cussed rather coarsely.

Regardless of my struggle to accept the different theological traditions, I began to learn how to critically engage with my own faith. I started to realise that certain practices I accepted as doctrines, were in fact fabricated by humans. That unleashed a colossal process of examining my faith that would span over the next three years of theological studies.

• • •

The struggle to understand my sexual and emotional urges continued during my studies. The intensity of my desire for male physical and emotional intimacy grew stronger. Belgian men seemed more oriented to one-night stands and less focused on friendships. Sometimes I wouldn't be interested in sex – just wanted to be held and caressed – but that was the only way I could get it.

Some men however, were quite charming and interesting, but just as with Niels, I distanced myself once I started developing feelings for them. Every now and then, I met with Thomas, a Dutch Christian man who explored his sexuality in secret, as he didn't want his wife to know. I had met him in the Netherlands a few times, and because he had some indirect connections with my university because of his church, he wanted to visit me in Leuven.

I loved his tall build and his cordial smile. His Bonhoeffer metal-framed glasses gave him a scholarly flair. Despite his broken English, we always had great conversations about faith, our puzzling sexuality and scientific explorations.

Anxiously, I brought Thomas up to my room – worried about

revealing to my classmates my hidden adventurous life. With our legs interlocked, I rested my head on Thomas's shoulder, cuddling into his body. As he started to gently kiss me, Thomas began unbuttoning my lumberjack shirt, caressing my chest.

"Is this wrong, Alex? I mean, I *know* it is, but I don't feel it."

"I believe there are degrees of wrongs, this being benign. It makes my heart sing." I touched his scruffy beard. "I don't feel this is sexual ... just giving each other the attention we both crave."

Thomas took my hand into his and looked away for a second. "I am trying to fight the urges, Alex. I love my wife ... more than you can imagi –"

I put my finger on his lips, trying to curb the avalanche of emotions . "I know you do ... the fact that we haven't had sex says a lot about your commitment to her."

He looked back at me, fighting back tears. "You have no idea how hard it is, when I crave a masculine embrace more than anything ..."

"Oh, believe me ... I do. Most days I live on ghosts from the past, trying to remember how it felt when someone touched me. But I am committed to *this* now," pointing towards the building, as if to mean the university itself.

Gently pulling my head towards his chest, Thomas said murmuring, "Let's just enjoy each other's company for a while. I'd love that."

Inebriated with the ecstatic feelings, I barely heard the rat-a-tat on the door. I recognised the handyman's voice – employed by the university to do repairs to the Peda. As he had a master key to my room, I ran towards the door and inserted my own key so that he couldn't enter. Both Thomas and I were shirtless and flustered.

As I tried to think of an excuse why I couldn't let him in, I put on my shirt calming myself. When the handyman finally came in, Thomas sat dressed and sipping from his tea, nonchalantly.

"This is Thomas, a friend of mine from Den Helder. He came to pay me a visit," I said, barely finding my words in Dutch.

They exchanged pleasantries. "How did you guys meet?" The handyman said looking at the electricity panel next to the couch.

I noticed Thomas struggling to find an answer. "We met at a *social* event in The Hague last summer," he mumbled. That was indeed where we met, being *social*.

The handyman gave me a funny look. "I replaced the broken fuse." Just as he was about to leave, he asked, "Why was the room locked?"

"I ... uhm ... always keep the door locked ... because of the cold. It seals better when it's locked." It was true; I couldn't believe where the explanation came from, though.

"That was a good save." Thomas opened his arms and gave me a long hug. "I should also go."

Back in my room, I couldn't believe what had happened. I began creating countless future scenarios in which I would be expelled once the incident reached the Dean. I knew I had the chance to explain, but the possibility of my secret being out in the open terrified me.

•   •   •

I uninstalled the gay apps and decided to talk with someone from university about my predicament. After a conversation with two of my lecturers, they told me about a secret group of students that struggled with their sexuality.

I was ecstatic to find other people like me at the university. The group offered a space for me to share my tumultuous inner life and the struggle to fit in. I was embraced with open arms and loved just as I was by people who loved God with all their hearts.

One of the guys mentioned that he was keeping himself sexually pure for his marriage with a man. That was still too heavy a concept for me to assimilate. I blamed his Dutchness for the freedom of his conscience, and secretly I envied him – I wanted his resolute mind.

Months after I first joined the group, I felt an increasing peace coming over me. Beginning to consider myself a 'normal' person, I decided to try embracing my own sexuality with all its messy history. I prayed that God would bring people into my life to help me reconcile the conflicting aspects of who I was.

A ROMANIAN
AFFAIR

IMMERSED IN THEOLOGICAL EXPLORATIONS during the spring of 2016, I found myself daydreaming about my time at the Bible school and the beauty of Sibiu. I knew how wonderful the city would be that time of year, adorned with a plethora of flowers. Because the Easter break was just around the corner, I decided to pay Mathilde a visit. She was elated to hear that we'd see each other again after such a long time.

Sibiu was as charming as ever. Piaţa Mare, the ground square surrounded by Baroque style buildings, had been my favourite place to unwind during my time at the Bible school. Untroubled by the constant rush of people passing by, I always thought I was transposed in an era of myth and fantasy.

I spent most of the time with Mathilde, catching up on past years. We went to our favourite Italian restaurant where I'd eaten the best pizzas.

"How have you been, *really?*" she asked, looking deep into my eyes.

Put on the spot, I didn't know how to respond …so much

had happened since the last time I saw her. "Oh, you know …
the existential struggle of finding oneself."

Mathilde raised an eyebrow. "Have you … found yourself?"

"To be honest, I'm not sure. I've known love in a way that I
never did befo–"

"With a man … you mean …"

"Yes, several." I broke the eye contact, trying to cut the pizza
slice in half. I felt a sudden surge of guilt – it didn't feel like
it originated in my heart. Looking at Mathilde's expression, I
realised it was vicarious.

"How have you reconciled that with your faith?" Her voice
dropped an octave.

"I haven't. I simply dived into it. There were moments, M,
when life seemed perfect, followed by bouts of guilt and shame.
I felt safe in the arms of a man, loved, even … redeemed."

"Oh, don't be naïve. You know *who* redeemed you. I have
prayed every *single* day for you. I love you with all my strength,
Alex, but you know I will never support you in what you do."
She shifted slightly in her chair. "I'm worried that the pressure
will make you do foolish things. Look what happened to
Stephan …"

I became annoyed with the direction of the conversation.
"Your brother had schizophrenia, M-A-T-H-I-L-D-E. I am
GAY." The words came out like a curse, as if I had spat from
my mouth; too acid.

We looked around, our faces becoming red. Heads turned.
I wanted the earth to open up and swallow me. Whispering
almost, she said, "A lot of people of *your kind* killed themselves,
Alex. This is serious."

"And you think I don't know that. I'm the one carrying this

curse, remember?" I realised my voice sounded too harsh. "I'm sorry, I didn't mean to have such a heated conversation."

Mathilde grabbed my hand and caressed it gently. "I know. I just want to make sure you don't hurt yourself. You have a good heart, Alex."

I managed a brief smile, "Thank you. I know you mean well. I wouldn't be here if I wasn't convinced of that. Anyway … mama Lupu sends you greetings." I tried to change the subject – I couldn't deal with the criticism anymore.

The first Sunday after I arrived in Sibiu, we decided to go to the church affiliated to the Bible school, so that I could see other old friends. On the way to Schellenberg, Mathilde said that she needed to pick someone up. When Bianca jumped into the car, I noticed right away an easiness about her.

"So, you're a poet, Mathilde told me," she said.

"Ah, you talked about me?" I looked at Mathilde, trying to hide her grin by looking at traffic.

"We girls talk about a lot of things." She pulled her body closer to the front seats.

"I do write sometimes. Not that often anymore, with my university." I looked back for a second and noticed curiosity etched on her face like a theatre mask. "My free time is taken up by photography now. I have a constant influx of clients … I'm very blessed."

"Combining pleasure with business, eh? Similar to me." I saw her glancing at children playing next to their mother at the lights. "Being an educator for me is both pleasure and work. I cannot wait to be a mum."

I felt she wanted to continue that idea, but she must have realised she was talking to a stranger. "I always wanted to be a father. I want my first to be a girl."

Mathilde looked at me for a second, burying her eyebrows into her eye sockets. "That escalated fast."

"We are all deep thinkers here, M! Don't tell me you haven't thought about having ki–" I realised too late how much that sentence must have hurt her. I had been so focused on my past and on my hurt that I'd forgotten about her own trauma.

Bianca sensed the tension. "Anyway, we are almost at the church … I will bombard you with questions after."

● ● ●

I loved being back in that church. Seeing so many familiar faces, my heart was filled with happiness and gratitude. I noticed one of my crushes from years ago was the lead singer in the band leading the worship. I smiled at her as our glances met. We'd never exchanged more than a few words during those three years of studies. She was out of my league, and I'd learnt to accept that.

As was the custom in Romanian Brethren churches, during the time of congregational prayer, the members of the church had the freedom to pray out loud, guided by a theme suggested by the liturgist. I began praying, overwhelmed by the coalescence of emotions inside me: "Father, I am so grateful for being able to see my church family again, after so many years. Thank You for enabling the fostering of faith in this church. I am so grateful for the fellowship we enjoy as believers, made possible by the love of Jesus. Amen." I noticed how heads were turning, when they recognised my voice.

After the service, I could think only about Bianca. As I was talking to my old friends, I kept an eye on the way she interacted with the people from church. She looked so comfortable in her own skin, so full of exuberance and charm. When she smiled, my heart was electrified.

On the way back home, after dropping Bianca at her place, Mathilde looked at me and with a teasing smile she said: "You like her, don't you?" The grin on my face perfectly reflected what was going on inside. I wanted to know everything about this enigmatic young woman.

The way her long dark brown hair moved in the breeze, reminded me of the trees in the forest where I spent my summers growing up. There was something so primal in the way she touched her hair every time she looked at me. I wanted to reach out, and push strands of it behind her ear.

* * *

The following Monday, I took the train to Cislău to visit my family. That same evening, using my excellent Facebook stalking techniques, I found Bianca's profile, and sent her a friend request. When she accepted it, I knew our journey of mutual discovery had begun.

After numerous conversations, she admitted that the warmth of my prayer in church in Schellenberg was the tipping point; her attraction to me took root in her heart. Every day I fell in love with her a little more. Lurking behind every flutter of the butterflies in my stomach, was the doubt that my affection for Bianca wasn't genuine. *You are fooling yourself, Alex! You aren't going to be an authentic husband. She needs a real man in bed, not a poponar.*

I thoroughly relished the feeling of 'normality' when telling people that I had a girlfriend. I was so sick of my grandmother saying: "You still don't have yourself a woman, do you? The clock is ticking, *Alexuț!*" I couldn't wait to parade Bianca in front of everyone.

• • •

Once back in Leuven, my conversations with Bianca continued; the depth of our friendship and closeness increased. I decided to book another flight two months later, after my exam week.

Despite of my difficulties with the Dutch language, I passed all the exams for that semester, which meant I could spend two months in Romania with Bianca. One evening, I wrote a poem for her called *Meeting*:

> I met your smile when I'd become immune to surprise –
> So fragile, yet so full of the exuberance of life, uncharted.
> You overwhelm my eyes with charm and guise –
> And rob my mind of thoughts and leave me
> faint-hearted.
>
> I met your voice when my life was rooted
> in a deafening hush –
> Piercing, sealing my thoughts with an alien sound,
> Shutting them down and making them blush
> Aware of the tune and the chords they have found.

Flying into Cluj, I loved the idea of spending an extended time in Transylvania – the culture of the people had won me over, no matter how much I loved the geography of southern Romania. Bianca met me at the airport, and we then took a bus to Sibiu. For the first time in my life, I held the hand of someone I loved without feeling ashamed. From time to time, I looked at her, catching her gaze for a couple of seconds.

I knew I had to tell Bianca about my complicated sexuality. I didn't leave out any important detail that she needed to know. I'd never felt so emotionally naked in my entire life. Not even Kees and Willem got such a deep insight into what had happened with me, and into who I was.

After my one-hour long monologue, she asked me a question that pierced through my shield: "Alex, will you love me and commit yourself to this relationship with all your strength?"

"Bia," looking deep into her eyes, "I do … I wouldn't be here if I didn't."

She smiled and looked at me, "That's all I need to know. Who you have been, it has already been forgiven."

I collected my face into a knot. "It won't be easy, you know that right?"

"I do. But if I know you love me and you're loyal to our relationship, we can face it together. You won't have to be alone anymore."

I loved her for that – she sounded so mature and so genuine.

"Thank you, Bia. You are truly a blessing."

She put her head on my shoulder, looking outside the window at the green pastures rushing past us. "Had you envisioned this conversation differently?"

"My heart was pounding out of my chest. I thought you would shame me and reject me."

"Why would you think that?" She lifted her head and touched my cheek with her left palm. Her wonder seemed genuine.

"You have no idea how many people have reacted that way… as if I become a different person right before their eyes."

"Well, I won't be that person." She put her head back on

my shoulder, putting one hand across my torso, squeezing me slightly.

We spent the rest of the bus journey in silence, while our spirits were connecting on a deeper level, with every passing second.

That first weekend, before we headed towards the village where Bianca grew up and where her parents still lived, I stayed with her sister's family in Sibiu. Once I met Bianca's brother in law, the mythical reality I'd been living in for the past months exploded like a soap bubble.

The physical attraction towards him was so strong, it felt to me as destructive as a black hole. I couldn't stop looking at the little hairs peering out of his t-shirt and at his well-defined chest. My attraction to Bianca didn't possess this quality, and it scared me to death. The desire to touch her body didn't consume me with the same vigour as it did with his. *Lord, please help me disregard this physical attraction I feel for him. I want to solely focus on Bianca.*

* * *

I found solace in being with Bianca on our way to meet her parents. Not having her brother in law around, helped me work through the anger at my puzzling sexuality. Utterly ashamed for experiencing those feelings for a brother in Christ, I wanted to simply disappear for a couple of years. It seemed that not even my love for Bianca was powerful enough to help me overcome these feelings.

The nervousness of meeting her parents distracted me from my inner battle. Her youngest brother came to the train station and picked us up. Shy and peaceful, he had just turned eighteen that month.

While listening to the way he constructed his ideas into sentences, I was taken aback by his resemblance to my brother. Looking in the rear-view mirror he said mischievously: "Are you nervous, Alex? ... You don't have to worry; they won't bite the first time!"

Bianca's parents received me with open arms. Her dad's eyes held a fatherliness that instilled in me an instantaneous and deep sense of love for him. But like an ominous chant, her mother's voice awoke a disquietude in me that reminded me of my mother growing up. Despite her polite welcome, my visceral intuition told me to be cautious.

Beautifully positioned at the foot of a tree-covered hill, their house was attached to a barn. Sparsely furnished, the room I was given doubled as a guest room and storage space. After taking my luggage up to the room, I decided to go with Bianca on a stroll around the village.

A quintessential Transylvanian village most houses were united with ridiculously thick walls. Every house was painted in a different colour, and just as in my village, people had benches outside their gates. It felt intimate, especially since older people stood outside enjoying the evening sun, knitting woollen socks and gloves for their grandkids. I remembered when *Mămaia* would visit us in the beginning of November and would give my brother and me several pairs of woollen socks. By the end of February, they would already have holes in them from us wearing them so much, refusing to allow my mother to wash them.

The atmosphere hung heavy with a rural odour – every household had at least a cow and a couple of sheep. The asphalt was patched with fresh manure, its smell exacerbated by the July heat.

Bianca made small talk with every person she met on the street, proudly introducing me as her boyfriend. The nerves fell away, and for a while, my tumultuous past as well.

• • •

In our absence, Bianca's mother went up to my room, and noticed my Bible among my luggage. Rifling through it, she found a letter that Maya had given me a couple of years ago. I had been meaning to take it with me from the Netherlands to Belgium, but I'd forgotten to take it out. The short letter read as follows:

My dearest Alex,
   Our friendship has been constantly on my mind for the past months. I miss our Friday night conversations when you frantically went on about your dreams to build a house by the lake, somewhere in Constanța. I miss the way you made me laugh. I have been wondering whether we would have been happy living together, by the sea. You are right; having a yellow front door might be a good idea. I am just not so sure about the aubergine-painted walls, though.
   Last night I had a big argument with my mother because of my sister. I cannot take it any longer. I know you care so deeply for me and I miss your support. I cannot stand that woman anymore, Alex. I cannot wait to move to Bucharest and leave everything behind. My father doesn't want to get involved, even though he sees how much I'm hurting. There is no one I can talk to here, not even grandma.

I wish things were different, my dear. I wish you were different. I know you would've loved me with all your heart. I want so badly to give a hug right now and tell you that I love you. More than you know.

Always loving you,

Your Maya.

As she finished reading the letter, Bianca's mother phoned the rest of her children, telling them what she'd uncovered. Convinced that I was cheating on her daughter with Maya, her mission became to make sure Bianca and I wouldn't be together anymore.

Despite her discovery, she didn't say a word to me about the letter, during my stay with them those four days. The next morning, as we were having breakfast in the outdoor kitchen, Bianca's father began asking questions about my living situation in the Netherlands and Belgium.

"I have lived with two friends for four years. They pay my tuition fees and most of my living expenses in Belgium," I said warily.

"Are they believers?" He poured a glass of milk for himself and took a seat next to me. He reeked of stables and manure.

"They were raised Catholic, but they do not believe anymore." I tried to change the subject. "I think Kees still *flirts* with the idea of a Force in the universe, but not in the way we do."

"Why aren't they married if they are in their forties?" He stood up, put his empty glass on the kitchen counter, and looked at me like a bronze statue, unmoved.

"Because they are married to each other?" I sensed the tension building, Bianca looking at me, refusing to blink.

"You mean ... they are *poponari*?" he fumed.

"Yes, they are homosexuals. It is quite common in the Netherlands. And legal."

He stormed outside. *What have you done, Alex? Could you not have fabricated a half-truth? What's going to happen now?*

. . .

After thirty minutes, just as Bianca and I finished washing the dishes, both parents came back into the kitchen, noticeably distraught. For the next hour, I felt bombarded by question after question regarding my relationship with Kees and Willem. My character was scrutinised, and no matter what answer I gave, their reply was that I was living with "abominable people" – something that a *real* Christian should not feel comfortable with. *What if they figure out that you are also "abominable", Alex? You think you can hide that from them? You are such a fool!*

By the end of that morning, I was completely exhausted. After having been called a variety of bad names by two strangers who knew nothing about me, I was ready to go home. The last two days of my stay, our communication was reduced to small talk.

The day before we headed to Cislău, Bianca told me her life story. "I was engaged once, Alex. We were inseparable. There was no day when we did not see each other. He met me a few days after he had broken up with his ex, a girl I grew up with. I said *yes* when he proposed, without even thinking; I loved him with every fibre of my being. Two months after we got engaged, he went back to his ex, and got married after only five days. Their child was born prematurely, we were told, but I've always suspected that they slept together while we were still engaged." She broke into heartbreaking sobs.

Her face was etched with so much pain as she recounted

her previous relationship. Having been already engaged once, Bianca said that her family had lost confidence in her ability to choose the right man.

Soon after that weekend, I began to feel perturbed by the blunt interference of her siblings and parents. Bianca tried to assure me of their good intentions, but I couldn't shake off the inkling of what it was about to happen.

After she broke up with her fiancé, she started writing in a diary everything she would've normally said to a real boyfriend. Like writing a novel inspired by true events, Bianca began to create an imaginary future husband, based on her preferences and her Christian values. Her creation became her universe. When I came along, she had just projected *him* onto me, like a suit you wear to your wedding.

I didn't allow Bianca's confession to influence my opinion of her – I wanted to make our relationship work in spite of it, and of the experience with her parents. I was still inebriated with the fantasy of one day being a big happy family.

I had previously capitulated to the idea of never getting married, so I ceased to imagine that one day I would have to introduce my girlfriend to my parents. But now, it weighed on my mind like dark summer clouds. I dreaded the disapproval of my father – I knew it would feel like a wrecking ball.

The goodbyes from Bianca's parents felt glacial. The anti-climax of those days spent with them created ripples in my confidence. The seeds of doubt took root inside my heart.

"Did you talk to your parents before we left?" I asked, holding Bianca's hand tightly.

"Yes, just a bit. They didn't want to talk; my mother was feeling sick." She wiped the train's steamy window erratically. "I am afraid I've lost them, Alex."

"Why do you say that?"

"Because I saw it in my mother's eyes. Just the same as with my ex ...she didn't want to talk to me. They behaved horrendously. You know what my mother said?"

"Wh–"

"That I shouldn't see your parents. Why can't they just be *happy* for me?" Her head fell into her crossed arms, leaning into the front seat, as the other passengers looked towards us.

I felt embarrassed and sad at the same time. "Then I shouldn't talk about my nerves. I am so anxious."

"That they wouldn't like me?"

"Yes ... maybe ... I don't know. I mean you're gorgeous, but they're not."

"They cannot be as bad as my parents." She smiled and wiped away her tears. "Wake me up when we get close. I need to rest a bit."

      • • •

My mother adored Bianca. Having similar personalities, they could talk endlessly about gardening, cooking, and their mutual love for children. My father was reserved in his judgement about her – creating a fragile sense of harmony between us. He was polite in conversations, and made sure Bianca felt at home. I adored showing her the places I loved in my village. However, I couldn't understand my reservation to take her to my secret spot under the willow tree. *What if she is not the one? I'll have to be absolutely sure first.*

I didn't want to stay longer than four days with my parents. Every corner of the street and every house reminded me of my past. The sty called to my mind scenes where little Alex became the victim of lust and wickedness. The earth I was stepping on had the same dust impregnated with the tears of a child beaten by the very man who should have protected him.

In the evening, we went walking, praying and telling each other how our day went.

"I love doing this with you, Alex. I feel protected next to you." Her eyes were glistening in the light of the streetlamps.

I couldn't believe that I could give someone such a feeling. "You do? Why?"

"You have this warm energy about you that tells me that you'll do anything to protect me. I knew that from the moment I stepped into Mathilde's car all those months ago." She stopped walking, tiptoed and gave me a kiss on the cheek.

"And that?"

"I haven't been this happy in a very long time, Alex. Can I call you *strawberry*?" She began laughing.

"Shh ... you'll wake the neighbours."

She giggled.

"Why strawberry?"

"It's my favourite fruit ... and you are my favourite person, it *seems* ... so why not?"

I lifted my shoulders and let them fall slowly. "Yes, I guess you can. I will call you *Acanbi*!"

"What's that?"

"It's an anagram. I mixed the letters of your name to form a new one ... a special one ... like you." I gave her a kiss on the cheek.

"Wow. I love it. But promise only when we are on our own. I want it to be our secret."

"Okay ... My beautiful *Acanbi*."

• • •

The day before we went back to Sibiu, I took Bianca to the bridge where I heard God's voice for the first time. Subconsciously, I wanted to bring her to the place I wanted to end my life to prove to my inner demons that their power doesn't have a hold over me. We took some photographs and posted them on Facebook.

Bianca hugged me from behind as I leaned against the balustrade. She planted a kiss on my neck. "Thank you for bringing me here. I feel I am part of that future God promised you."

I turned around and took her into my arms, staring into her eyes. "You are my beautiful blessing." I gave a kiss on her forehead.

"He knew about the man you'd become, Alex."

"There are so many moments when I doubt all that, *Acanbi*. My manhood … my future … my purpose. What is a man without a purpose?"

"I'll be your purpose. And you'll be mine."

"That's right. I'm sorry. I don't know what came over me. Shall we go back? We have some packing to do."

* * *

Once in Transylvania, Bianca went to a children's summer camp to Budila. (She'd spend most of her holiday volunteering for summer camp planning and leadership. "I cannot get enough of being around children," she said to me before she stepped into the bus). I welcomed the opportunity to spend a couple of days on my own, analysing everything that had happened those past two weeks. I knew that the relationship with her parents would probably never be cordial, nor civil. The dream of finally having a loving father, shattered as fast as their love for me.

Once Bianca finished with her first summer camp, I went

to Budila to help her with a second camp she'd organised. I volunteered to be a leader for boys from ten to thirteen. I loved our evening strolls around the village, after the daily program, talking about what had happened during the day, and then praying together.

One evening, as we were sitting on a bench next to the bank of the river, Bianca confessed that her mother had read my letter and that her entire family knew about me and Maya. I felt incredibly violated. The fact that *she* knew about it all this time, hurt me the most. That flame inside my heart that kept my love for her burning, began flickering.

Despite still having another two weeks left in Romania, I left sooner. I needed time on my own, without her jealous mother and her challenging family. The tranquillity of Leuven gave me the peace I needed.

• • •

I thought that it would be a brilliant surprise for Bianca to celebrate her birthday in the Netherlands. I was so excited to introduce her to Kees and Willem and to the rest of my Dutch family. But when I called her parents to tell them about my surprise for her, they said that they wouldn't allow her to be in another country with me, unless we were engaged. *How could they want us to be engaged, when they so blatantly hate me?*

Motivated by the fear of negative attention, they said that the engagement would protect their daughter's reputation. *Or theirs?*

I was certain I loved Bianca. Though I had a considerable amount of doubt, I regarded it as being caused by her family. A couple of hours later, I called her father back to ask him for his daughter's hand.

After a long delay, during which I could hear him whispering to his wife, he simply said, "Fine, Alex. You can ask our daughter to marry you." He then hung up, not giving me the chance to thank him.

It felt surreal, as if it wasn't me who wanted this to happen. I wasn't ready to be a husband, every fibre of my being knew it. *You're making a mistake My child. Even your own heart tells you that.* I recognised that voice inside my spirit, but the anticipation of happiness felt like lusting after a forbidden drug.

• • •

Two weeks before she arrived at Eindhoven airport, I bought a white-gold diamond ring, but struggled with the wait; so many complications with the order and the delivery. *This is an omen, Alex! You can still stop this charade.* I told myself that these things happen all the time, and I went on as planned.

When I saw her through the sliding doors, all my doubts and insecurities melted away. She abandoned herself into my arms, and I welcomed her in.

"Are you on your own?" I looked behind the sliding doors, jokingly.

"Who else?" Bianca asked.

"Your *brother*!"

"Very funny. No, I am alone and all yours."

"You will meet your host family first. They are lovely people. And then you will get to meet my Dutch family," I said buoyantly.

"I can't wait to meet them. I am sure I'll love them." Bianca looked at me and gave me another warm hug. I'd been craving the warmth of her infatuation with me. It felt so good to be desired.

• • •

Bianca loved meeting Kees and Willem, just as she'd hoped. The four of us had lunch, throwing questions back and forth like a game of badminton.

"I love your accent," said Willem, smiling. "You sound exactly like Alex when he first came to the Netherlands."

"Thank you, Willem. I had a good teacher for the past months." Bianca looked at me affectionately.

I took her hand into mine. "You know how much I love teaching language."

"Has Alex's changed then?" she asked.

Kees straightened his back and put his elbows on the table. "Yes, he sounds more Dutch nowadays. Which is not surprising after having lived with us … we've always spoken English with a Dutch accent."

"We thought that we'd take you to Breda this afternoon. That is where Alex studied for his degree …" said Willem.

"Unfinished …" interrupted Bianca, gently elbowing me.

"Sounds good. I'll show you all my favourite spots," I put the knife on the table glaring over at Kees and Willem. "We can let the *oldies* do the groceries," I laughed.

"Classy, Alex. I'd let you walk back if Bianca wasn't with you," teased Kees. "You two can get ready … we can clear this up."

• • •

I decided that the best place to propose to Bianca was at Efteling – a fantasy-themed amusement park in Kaatsheuvel, fifteen kilometres from Tilburg. The park was one of the first things

I saw when I moved to the Netherlands and it conquered my heart – I couldn't think of a better place to symbolise my desire to spend the rest of my life as her husband.

Under the pretext of showing her the things I loved in Tilburg, I convinced her to visit the amusement park. Because the day I chose was also Willem's birthday, Bianca wasn't surprised to hear that the grandparents, as well as Kees and Willem, would also join us. They were the most important people in my life, and I wanted them to witness my declaration of love to the woman with whom I wanted to build a future.

Last to leave the house, Kees said that he'd like to talk to me about something.

"Alex, are you sure you're not rushing into things?"

"What do you mean?" I asked him, impatiently.

"Are you *really* sure you want to propose to her? What about your *real* feelings?"

I felt he emphasised *real* as if my feelings for her weren't. "But I love her, Kees. I want to spend my whole life with her." I moved closer to the door.

"Don't get me wrong, Alex. I am not against your relationship with her … she looks like a lovely young woman. I am just concerned for you. This is not like with Chris. You are *proposing*, for goodness sake!"

"Oh, don't bring that up! Don't you think I don't know?"

"We are just concerned, Alex. That's all. It's all so hurried." Kees put his arms around me.

"You've discussed this with Willem?"

"Yes, last night when we were talking about your plans to propose." We both looked at each other perplexed. "You've know her only … what … six months?"

I unconsciously withdrew from his embrace, reaching the

front door. "I do appreciate your concern, but I think I've got this. My *real* feelings, as you call them, have nothing to do with this. I think they're waiting for us."

. . .

A Romanian friend who worked at Efteling had gained permission from the park managers, for me to propose before the four o'clock show of Raveleijn – a performance with five horse riders trying to free a village from the domination of the Count Olaf Grafhart and his five-headed fire-spitting dragon.

We walked into the packed amphitheatre – at least six hundred people waiting for the show to begin – and were ushered into the VIP area. I'd only told Kees and Willem my plans, so the grandparents thought that Kees must have surprised Willem with VIP tickets for his birthday.

With a microphone in one hand and the ring box in another, I knelt in front of Bianca, overwhelmed by nerves.

"Bianca, for the last few months, I have had the unbelievable privilege of getting to know the most amazing woman I have ever met … you. I cannot imagine my future without you being part of it." I could see her face slowly turning red and her eyes opening up, teary. "Would you like to be my wife?" My voice was breaking.

She covered her mouth in disbelief, her left hand slowly shook. "Yes, Alex. I'd love to be your wife."

I gave the microphone to the organisers as the audience clapped and whistled. I finally gave her a long-awaited kiss. The show's organisers gave us a bottle of champagne and two glasses with the logo of the park embossed on them.

"*Gefeliciteerd*, Alex!" said *Oma*, Kees's mother, her voice trembling.

Opa hugged me and whispered in my ear, "Make her happy." He winked.

"*Gefeliciteerd*, Alex. We suspected nothing," added Willem's parents.

Kees and Willem embraced me tightly. They *seemed* happy, a tiny frown that lasted less than a second betraying Willem's smile.

And then, my own fear began plaguing my happiness. *What have you done, Alex?* A realisation clouded my thinking. Small panic attacks rippled through my body. I got up and ran seeking solace in the restroom. I began crying breathlessly. *Father, I am not so sure I made the right choice! I can't go back to the way things were this morning. Am I really meant to be a husband? How Lord? How can I ever be a husband with those other unwanted attractions?*

Blaming proposal nerves, Bianca did not suspect what was happening inside of my mind. I knew I had to stop worrying, so I buried my feelings so deep I wouldn't be tempted to unearth them.

The weekend after the proposal, we had the *Boertjesdag* celebration with Kees' extended family. For the first time in five years, I was no longer unaccompanied. Everyone was so excited for us and their happiness became my drug, numbing my conflicting emotions. Bianca showed off her ring to my Dutch family, bursting with joy and pride.

• • •

Kees suggested we go to Heusden to take engagement photographs. It was a beautiful sunny autumn afternoon with the trees still adorned with multi-coloured leaves. Years before, infatuated with Xander, I couldn't have imagined that I would have pictures taken for my engagement, *with a woman.*

When Kees asked us to pose kissing, something inside me snapped. I couldn't kiss her. I blamed my past, but I knew that was only an excuse. Bianca drew back in disappointment, though she knew I didn't like to express my love in public, except for holding hands.

• • •

She cried when I said goodbye to her at the airport, but I was secretly relieved. I still loved her, but I needed space, away from her and the reminder that I was engaged to be married.

The weeks after Bianca returned to Romania, we started fighting. Her family trying to convince her that she'd made a big mistake. Having been asked to pick a side, Bianca decided to stand by her decision to get married. She lost her parents' support entirely.

"I will stand by you no matter what, Alex." I could hear her silent sobs through the phone.

"I am so sorry, *Acanbi.* I wish they could see our love is true." My heart cried seeing Bianca suffering that way.

"Why can't they just accept that some people are different? And that we can't change them."

I frowned. "What do you mean?"

"We had a fight last night because I told them how lovely Kees and Willem were to me when I visited you. They didn't want to hear that. They said you *bewitched* me. As if I am some sort of small stupid little girl. I wish you were here with me."

"Hold on, love ... just for two months. We'll see each other again. I promise."

"You know what my brother said?"

"What?" I could feel my blood pressure rising.

"He said why ... would I ... want to be part ... of a family of ... drunkards and sluts." She almost spat the words in between the sobs.

I could hardly contain my fury. "Maybe he should focus on his own family. At least mine doesn't pretend to be *saved*." I surprised myself with how defensive I sounded, not sure I was affected by what he'd said about my family, or simply because he couldn't help but interfere.

"I am so sick of it, Alex."

"I know. So am I. Why don't you have a rest and we can video chat later?"

. . .

Two days later, as I was about to go for a stroll in the forest, I saw a message from Bianca on my phone:

Alex,
I cannot do this any longer.
There is nothing of God in our relationship and I am losing all my friends because of you.
My family has abandoned me, and I cannot live without their love. I hope your faith will get you through the disappointment.
I hope to see you in heaven.

When I tried to call her, I realised she'd blocked me on all social media platforms. Unable to even send a reply, my heart was flooded with remorse. I clung onto those feelings for the next couple of days because I was ashamed to admit that I was happy. My inner world was unshackled, and I regained my freedom. I didn't have to fight gaining the trust of future in-laws and I didn't need to worry whether I'd be able to have sex with my future wife. *You can breathe now.*

*   *   *

A few hours after I'd uploaded a blogpost on my website talking about my experience with the breakup, I received a text from Bianca on my Skype account demanding that I delete what I'd written, otherwise she would tell all my friends in Sibiu about my secret. She was threatening to *out* me.

The more I reread her reply, the darker my beautiful image of Bianca became. I fought the bitterness with quixotic strength. *Father, help me forgive and forget her. I want it all gone.*

As a monument, meant to immortalise my acquiescence, I wrote a poem that afternoon, entitled *Paucity of memories*:

> You deprived my eyes of the silhouette of your smile
> And of the streams of your corrugated vowels
> When my name took off – released from your lips, for a while –
> Nesting with your feral beasts and your owls.
>
> You bereave my thoughts
> Time erects dams of a thousand feet high.
> I swim in a lake
> Filled with the echo of a precious goodbye.

For the next couple of months, I threw myself into my studies. I opened the door to deeper friendships with the students living in the dorm. I couldn't wait to graduate so I could move out of Belgium. The city of Leuven felt dead to me most of the time, unable to satisfy my desire to be solaced, even though I didn't know what *that* looked like.

I didn't want to go back to the Netherlands either. I abhorred the idea of being embraced by Kees and Willem with an attitude of *I told you so*. Kees had asked whether my *erratic* decision wasn't just a desperate message to the world that I wasn't gay. I wasn't entirely convinced that he was wrong.

. . .

Surrendering to the idea that I'd probably never find a woman to marry, I became satisfied with online interactions with gay men. Like a cheap substitute for intimacy, I learnt to be gratified with the transient connection offered by sexting. My body became the currency of that exchange, as well as its most avid consumer.

Little did I know that life had another surprise in store for me in the autumn of 2017.

BLOSSOMS

THE OATH

ON 28 SEPTEMBER 2017, life was about to take an unforeseeable turn. Overwhelmed with lethargy, I logged onto my
gay forum account, hoping that I'd find someone to talk to
before I went to bed. Rory, an Irish guy living in Australia, was
online. I decided to send him a message. We had been chatting
on-and-off for the past two years, but never deeper than talking
about how our day had been.

There was something serendipitous about that evening.
Surprisingly, Rory seemed to be in a garrulous mood. Texting
well into the hours of the morning, my attention was awakened.
I loved the way he meticulously revealed parts of his life – like
unpeeling an onion. Just before I went to sleep, we exchanged
phone numbers.

A little flame inside me rekindled. Once we started to use
iMessage, we texted every day. I couldn't stem the desire to get
to know him better. Six weeks later, we began having hour-long
conversations on FaceTime.

● ● ●

It became increasingly hard to concentrate during my lectures as I daydreamt about how life would look living with Rory, in Australia. Most days I felt overwhelmed with the uncertainty of the future, as that was my last year at the university. The curriculum demanded that I'd have an internship in the second half of the first semester – in a church or religious organisation. One morning, as I was drinking a cup of tea on the veranda, I was animated by a wild idea – combining visiting Rory with doing my internship in Canberra.

My thumb shook uncontrollably as I was about to dial Rory. "What would you say if I applied for a work placement in Canberra and so, be able to … see you?" Uttering the words gave me goosebumps.

"That would be good. Unexpected, but good."

An awkward silence fell over us for a few seconds. "Are you sure you are okay with it?"

"Yes. Sorry, Alex. I am not that used to surprises. I am *thrilled.*" The words came out forced, unconvincingly.

His voice threw me off a little, but I was willing to go on with my plan. "Perfect. I will see to it."

In the following days, I sent emails to all Baptist churches in Canberra inquiring whether they would like to offer me a three-month internship opportunity. *Father, I know that if You want me to go to Australia, I will get an answer from one of the ministers.*

Less than a week later, Mike, the pastor from one of the Baptist churches in Canberra replied to my email. He seemed enthusiastic about the prospect of having me in his church as an intern.

After the university approved my request, Rory and I worked extensively on my visa application. I simply couldn't believe that I was going to see him in less than three months. Our love was real. I didn't want to think about the implications of my emotions for Rory. The panic attacks assaulted my mind like a battering ram. Later, I'd realise that, in fact, my own capacity for loving was in fact a Trojan horse that would besiege my existence.

* * *

During one of the tutorials, the guest lecturer spoke about a lay preacher in his church who arrived at the conclusion that God allowed him to marry another man. I'd read about that position in my private study of the Bible, but it never made such an impact as during that class.

After the lecture, I asked him if I could talk to him in private about this issue. Going into an empty classroom, he argued that as long as one has the seal of approval from the Holy Spirit in being in a sexual relationship with a person of the same sex, then that union is morally good. For the first time in my life, I began to doubt my theological foundation regarding my sexual ethics.

A couple of weeks later, after I turned off the alarm, I noticed a text from Rory. It was a poem with the title *Horizon*:

The infinite horizon beckons me
Anchoring my feet in the sand,
Pulling my gaze to a promise of calm between its two worlds.

The ocean's heart beats onto the shore.
Its metronomic certainty resonates
Promising a place of safety and a happiness that now seems muted.

But then its hold is broken as you take my hand
And I turn to see the horizon reflected in your eyes.
In that moment, I feel unimaginable happiness
In the knowledge that I am loved
And that we share a love that makes me complete.
For the infinite horizon is naught
Compared to the infinite love I have for you.

Tears of happiness flooded my eyes. No one had ever written a poem for me before. I desired Rory's embrace with my entire being, just to be able to look him in the eyes and tell him that I loved him. Thinking about his eyes, I wrote a poem for him, entitled *Canberran Glances*:

Are those the eyes that melt my heart, making it bloom?
Lifting my soul on wings of comely smiles?
Are those the lips that incarnate my name,
across the miles?
Feeding my mind with their aural perfume?

Come and intertwine your fingers with mine
On the beach whose sand carries our footprints
and weight.
Arid landscapes that bear my name and design
Have been immersed in the ocean of fate.
I long for the marriage of our glances to start;
Let your thoughts in my eyes radiate
Allowing your love to grow roots in my heart.

The war inside my mind had begun. I knew that even though I desired with all my strength to accept my lecturer's perspective, something inside told me it wasn't right. It wasn't about particular Bible verses that prohibited sex between men, but the entire narrative of creation reflected the original design of the union between feminine and masculine.

Bursting into tears while praying, one evening before going to sleep, I begged God: *Father, if I am to be celibate for the rest of my life, please allow me to feel loved by a man, by Rory, in every sense of the word. Allow me to delight in the love of a man one last time. I promise that after those three months in Australia, I will never want to be in a relationship with a man.*

My mind found rest after my prayer that night. The threat of panic attacks disappeared. All I had to do was to keep my promise.

Two weeks before 4 February – when I would fly to Australia – Rory sent me an email with something he had written about how he imagined our first reunion:

My mind stirs. My brain and body still in paralysis, trapped between the worlds of sleep and consciousness. A dream continues to resonate, the same dream that reruns every night. A dream of a journey with no end.

As I turn my head, shards of sunlight pierce my eyelids and fire my brain into life. Almost instantly, a moment of clarity – the journey in my dream has no end because its completion can only be realised by my conscious mind, body and spirit. And that ending will be realised today. For today is the day of Arrival.

Now I need to fill the hours. But the clock stands seemingly still, barely moving between glances. I prepare for the journey, but every action, every thought is infused by events to come. Events I have imagined, anticipated and rehearsed in my mind. They play out in my head one last time and make the tortuous last hours almost bearable.

At last, the journey begins. Along a road whose end will change my life forever. I use music to mask my thoughts and emotions. But every song seems to have been written for me, written for this day, written for this moment. Songs that have drawn on the hope, love and longing in my mind.

Then, I am there. The place of Arrival.

A hub of constant movement. Faces looking upwards towards the sky. Heads craned towards glowing screens that bring the promise of reunion. Eyes looking at watches, waiting. We wait together, in a mutual, unspoken union of anticipation and excitement.

But I feel so alone in the throng, my face masking the internal turmoil.

A robotic voice cuts through the cacophony, announcing the Arrival and like sheep, the crowd migrates as one. I am carried along, my breathing laboured as if at the end of a marathon. Collective emotions heighten as human forms emerge in the distance. I struggle to maintain my composure as I realise that the rehearsals that have replayed in my mind of this moment have not prepared me for this journey's end. The intense longing I feel as I wait in those final seconds could not be rehearsed, imagined or prepared for.

And then, amongst the indistinguishable faces, you are there.

My mind tells me that it cannot be true. But then our eyes meet, and I know that my whole life has been a rehearsal for this moment. My heart wants to burst through my chest as I see your smile. It takes all my physical energy to move my feet and walk to you. All the time, our eyes remain connected and suddenly we are but a few steps apart.

My hand reaches out. Our palms touch and our hands entwine. Electricity explodes through my body and I open my arms. You fall into me and I will time to stand still because I want this moment to last forever. The moment I fell in love.

We pull apart and I look in your eyes and I know there is only one thing to say: Alex, I love you.

I couldn't explain the emotions streaming through my body. Rory's love and desire to see me seemed as real as the air I breathed. I couldn't stop thinking about how electrifying our first meeting would be. I could hardly concentrate on anything else those last days.

Before I stepped into the plane, I wrote a short poetic reply:

I miss your eyes even before seeing them. That azure blue that covers my landscapes with its nuances inspired by the summer skies, lures me into a dance on Irish meadows. I lose the sense of time whenever I build bridges between my eyes and yours; I cannot find my way home, but I loiter on the intricate highways of your soul.

I miss your soft hands even before feeling them. Their tender touch and silky textures redefine the geography of my skin. I am enchanted by the music made by your fingers every time you caress my arm. I want my skin to be covered in millions of fingerprints left by your touch.

I miss your embrace even though you have never hugged me. I long for that warmth that dissolves any negative thought with its intensity. I want to watch the sunset lost in your arms. Oh, how I miss that unfelt embrace.

I miss tomorrow while contemplating the fact that you are always 10 hours closer to that kiss I so deeply desire.

● ● ●

I arrived at ten in the evening at Sydney airport. Passing through the sliding doors I could see Rory pacing up and down in the waiting area. Smiling, he embraced me, and gave me a kiss on my cheek. It felt sublime.

"Welcome to Australia," he almost shouted.

"Thank you. You have no idea how amazing is to finally see you," I grinned.

"It is just as intense as in my essay. You look very handsome," he whispered in my ear.

I blushed. "And so do you." I brushed his hand, grabbing my suitcase handle. My body electrified. "The anticipation killed me. It did help having WiFi on the plane."

"Yes. It helped me as well. Otherwise, I would have worried the entire twenty-seven-hour journey. I got you some presents; I have them in the car … your Australian survival kit."

Walking towards the car park, I said jokingly, "You are shorter than me."

"Is that a deal breaker?" he laughed.

"No, I just had this weird expectation that Irish men are rather tall."

"Sorry, I can't do anything about that!" When we reached the car, he took a big box out of the boot.

I unwrapped it. "Wow, I cannot believe you got me the leather bag. Did you have it sent all the way from Belgium?"

"Yes. I spoke to a lady on the phone about buying it. She talked just like you!" He laughed, imitating my accent.

I gave him a hug. "Thank you, it's so lovely." The rest of the *kit* consisted of: a small book with Aussie slang, a button that when pressed, delivered Australian phrases in a broad Aussie accent, a Eucalyptus lip balm (I still have no idea why), and a stubby holder.

Listening to our favourite playlist – songs we had been compiling – and talking about the flight, made the journey to Canberra seem less than three hours. There was still so much to get to know about each other. We shared no awkward moments, it felt as if I was meeting an old friend.

• • •

Getting used to living with Rory was easy. He was at work most of the day, allowing me to take in the change of scenery. Everything about Australia was different. I absolutely disliked the time zone. When I felt lonely during the day and wanted to chat with my friends in Europe, I soon realised that they were sleeping; just as I was about to go to bed, I'd be flooded with messages. We always seemed out of sync.

The house was *gezellig* (my all-time favourite Dutch word – closest translation would be *cosy*). Traces of Rory lingered in absolutely every corner. A lover of music, hundreds of CDs and DVDs were alphabetically displayed on white wooden shelves in the living room, lounge room, bedroom – frankly, everywhere. East-facing, the bedroom was flooded with light in the morning, giving me hope and energy.

Ten days after I arrived in Canberra, Rory and I went for a weekend to Callala Bay, a small town on the south coast of New South Wales. We rented a beach cottage, only fifteen metres from the ocean.

The house was decorated in such a familial fashion, that I felt as if I'd come for a visit to my family home. The master bedroom faced the ocean, so in the evening I could hear the waves crashing onto the shore – like a primeval lullaby – and in the morning, I was woken up by sunbeams as the sun rose above the ocean.

Walking hand-in-hand on the white beach, I felt the happiest in my entire life; ethereally connected to that place. Some moments my heartbeats felt in sync with the rhythm of the ocean. Rory brightened seeing me so elated.

Eating fish and chips and drinking *Lazy Yak* with the man I loved, watching the stars appearing in the sky as the sounds of the waves lulled us into their symphony, I couldn't believe that I had ended up in this corner of paradise. God's love and goodness enveloped me. It wasn't a rationalisation anymore; the entire emotional landscape of my inner world was flooded with the light of His love.

• • •

Once the internship started, I made meaningful connections with the people in church. Our pastor Mike made me feel at home. The Tuesday-evening Bible study groups gave me the chance to build deeper friendships with my new faith family.

I most loved the ministry of the church with the elderly, every second Wednesday. Besides having chats and playing Scrabble together, I gave a five-minute speech meant to encourage them on their faith journey.

On a Friday morning, I joined Mike on a journey to Jervis Bay to watch a sport event that he was part of. Curious to know his perspective, I asked Mike what he thought of Christian same sex attracted men.

"I'm sure I am not alone in saying that being attracted to a man is sinful," he blurted, with a weird grin on his face. He seemed *almost* proud to declare that.

"What do you mean? Even the attraction itself? Not the act?"

"Yes. That's right. The presence of the attraction is indicative of the sinfulness in that man's life," he insisted, looking straight above the wheel.

I didn't know how to depersonalise the rest of the conversation. "But it seems that the man doesn't have any control over the attraction. It comes natural to him, just as *for us* being attracted to a woman comes natural."

"I simply refuse to believe that." He sounded adamant.

"What if that man is a Christian?" The question hovered close to the *fire*.

He looked directly into my eyes. "If I had such a man in my church, I wouldn't allow him to preach or to be part of the worship team. Such man is living in sin."

Masking my anger and disappointment, I asked, "How did you arrive at such a conclusion?" I needed some time to process what I'd just heard.

"I've always thought that. My theological education only confirmed my position. Why? What is your stand on this?"

I felt like a deer in the headlights. "I have been struggling with this matter for a long time now, mainly because I have so many gay friends. But I haven't reached a conclusion. I definitely can't accept your *opinion* that the attraction itself is sinful. Otherwise, Jesus Himself would be considered sinful ... the Bible says that He was tempted but He did not give in." My blood boiled.

Mike looked towards me again, frowning. "I don't think you can make that inference. His capacity to be tempted was pure, whils–"

"Exactly the same for us." I interrupted, aware of my reaction turning slightly passive-aggressive.

He grinned. "It seems we won't solve this one now. Shall we go through your sermon? We still have thirty minutes before we reach Jervis Bay."

I acquiesced, trying to concentrate on my breathing – I could feel the pulse in my throat throbbing. I admired Mike from the very beginning. He had a sophisticated way of expressing his thoughts, that only learned men had. The fact that he had a doctoral degree made me esteem him even more. But that morning, the pedestal toppled. I felt like a charlatan, pretending to be someone I wasn't.

After that day, every time I preached in front of the congregation, Mike's words echoed from every corner of my mind. I knew I couldn't expunge them unless I left the church, but that wasn't an option, at that time. Was I really responsible for my own instincts and proclivities even though I had no power over them?

• • •

Rory was supportive of my work with the church. He called himself a "non-practicing atheist", but he was curious about my faith. His questions were mostly related to the gospel and how God interacts with humans. Coming the first Sunday with me to church as a way of supporting me in kicking off with the internship, Rory decided to join me every Sunday after that. He seemed impressed with Mike's sermons and the warmth of the people during morning tea.

During dinner, we often had discussions about biblical characters, ethics and doctrines related to sexuality. One day, Rory came home bewildered by something that had happened to him during a lunchtime walk around Lake Burley Griffin. "Alex, as I was thinking about our conversation from yesterday about grace, I heard a voice inside my head saying *you are now ready to believe*! I was aflutter as I knew that was definitely not my own voice. What does it mean?"

It wasn't just a rhetorical question. Deep inside his heart he recognised the voice of his Father. Minutes later, Rory rested his head on his palms, his body curling like a question mark. Enraptured by the myriad of emotions, he simply said "I want to become a follower of Jesus!" We prayed together and sat in silence as we ruminated on what had happened.

I couldn't believe it. I had been praying for Rory, but my faith had been obliterated by doubt. He was an amazing man, full of compassion and concern for the world around him. I was so intrigued to see how his geniality would grow through the new reality of being a Christian.

I'd never loved another human being more that I came to love Rory. However, the new reality of him becoming a Christian, changed something inside me. All previous relationships and crushes melted into my besottedness with my Irish lover, but he suddenly became my brother. Every kiss and every caress seemed to defile our relationship – it felt almost as if its parameters had just been redefined. I struggled to connect with Rory sexually.

• • •

To my surprise, I came across a handful of Romanians in the church. Some were born in Romania and immigrated to Australia while others were Australians of Romanian descent. I loved being able to talk in my mother tongue with them deriding antipodean customs.

One Sunday after the church service, with five weeks left of my internship, while having morning tea, I was introduced to Isabel, a beautiful young woman with curly raven black hair, complementing a vanilla white knee-length dress. Charmed by her unassuming demeanour and suave voice, I wanted to get to know her better. She had a risible Romanian accent, ever so influenced by her Australian English albeit having been raised by Romanian parents. After meeting her a couple of times, it seemed that it could develop into something more than just friendship. I was aware that my romantic relationship with Rory would end once I went back to Europe. *Maybe Isabel would like to explore the idea of getting to know each other.*

Once I conceived those thoughts, I immediately felt paralysed by guilt. There I was, supposedly in love with Rory, thinking about having a relationship with a woman. I tried to rationalise it. *Well, you are thinking about a woman; that should sanctify that thought.* In the end it didn't, the guilt was present every time I'd look into Rory's eyes.

I explained to Rory that getting married to a woman and having my family might be a possibility in the future, he said, "Alex, I can't imagine your future without you being a father." I could hear sadness in his voice, as well as enthusiasm.

"What about *our* future?" I asked afraid of the answer.

"We knew this would be temporary. Besides, I'm not

interested in a relationship after you go back to Europe. I need to focus on my faith."

I couldn't believe the words coming out his mouth.

"But I'd like to come back," I said, taking his face into mine.

"I would like nothing more than living with you until you find and have your own family."

I started crying, overwhelmed by sadness.

"Don't cry, Alex. I knew *that* from the first time I saw you at the airport. I never told you this, but I've always had the feeling you'll be married one day and be a father to *Evangeline*, the daughter you always said you wanted."

I thought this would be the perfect moment to talk to him about Isabel. "There is a girl in church –"

"Isabel?" Rory interrupted, grinning. He elbowed me.

"How did you know?"

"I saw the way you look at her. I didn't mind … that's why I never told you I noticed it. If you think you need my permission to ask her out, you don't. Just be careful."

"Are you sure?" I was not entirely convinced he was genuine, afraid that he'd say that because it would make me happy.

"Yes. You have my *blessing*."

I decided to ask her whether she'd like to go out with me.

So many things made us utterly different: I had a free spirit; Isabel was still heavily influenced by her family. I loved getting to know new people and interact with the world around me; she was timorous and lacked confidence. I loved serving the Lord with all my talents and whenever I saw an opportunity; Isabel seemed more comfortable taking a step back. I appreciated her willingness and desire to serve other people. When the Romanian gang went to her place for a game night, she always made sure everyone was comfortable and well fed.

One Saturday afternoon, while having lunch with Isabel and her parents, we decided to tell them about our desire to get to know each other better, with the intention of a romantic relationship if we fell in love. Her mother was elated. After we all prayed, I began telling them about my story, growing up in Romania. I noticed her father trying to hide his silent sobbing. I loved him all the more for having been moved by my childhood suffering.

Next weekend, Isabel and I spent a weekend with her parents at their place on the coast. Her mum's cooking reminded me of the dishes my mum used to make growing up. Her father was reserved in showing affection, but I knew he liked me from the hour-long conversations we had about biblical theology and its doctrines.

I loved Isabel's family – they made me feel as if I'd always belonged to them. I truly felt that her dad could become the father I'd never had. We spent countless hours playing Rook – an American card game – and strolling on the beach.

But despite the amazing time I was having with Isabel and with her parents, my heart was not animated by the idea of being married to her, yet. Whilst I enjoyed being in her company, I realised that the physical attraction and emotional connection that I would've expected, just wasn't there. Further exacerbating my doubt, Isabel became increasingly nervous about my desire to work as a pastor in the near future. Sometimes, I got the impression that she wished I'd never get a job in church ministry.

I could hear the echoes of the words Rory told me "I've always had the feeling you'll be married one day and be a father to *Evangeline*," but not even his confidence could reassure me that that those things would ever happen. After a couple of days of asking God's wisdom in prayer, I knew inside my heart that I shouldn't get married, yet. We were on our way to her parents, so I decided to tell her.

She didn't take it the way I expected. Unconsciously I had hoped that she'd received the same answer, but she got the exact opposite.

"Am I not good for you, Alex? What's wrong with me?"

"You know it's not about that, Isabel. Some people are meant to be together, others aren't. I *know* that we fall in the latter category."

"But how have I received a different answer from God?" Her tone changed. She looked at me for a second, and then concentrated on the traffic.

Fear took hold as she swerved between cars. "I don't know, Isabel. One of us might be wrong …"

She took the sharp corners of the Macquarie Pass too fast.

"Let's not tell them today. Let me have some time to process *this*," Isabel bellowed.

"Are you sure? They'll notice."

"I'll come up with a reason." Her right eye twitched. "Don't you worry about me."

I knew better but to argue. I looked out the window to the scenery, much greener than in Canberra, and I could almost smell the salty air coming from the ocean.

The next morning, while Isabel and I were having breakfast with her parents, I knew I couldn't hide what was going on inside me. I was convinced I wasn't ready to get married and I couldn't give them hope anymore.

Her parents argued that they thought the opposite, just as Isabel. Her mum could already envision the wedding. All of a sudden, from the pedestalled status I had seconds before, I was downgraded to 'a man who didn't have a close relationship with God' – mainly because of my inability to sense the *real* will of God.

I didn't want to argue – I was done fighting. The rest of the weekend was tense and the conversations artificial. I had doubted whether to take a bus and go back to Canberra on my own, but Isabel convinced me to stay. She was hurting, but I didn't know how to console her. Strolling along the beach, on Sunday evening, I felt I had made the right decision. The waves seemed to smile and the tame heat of the evening sun caressed me like a parent's approval.

Isabel broke contact with me after that weekend. I stopped thinking about the prospect of getting married. It seemed that having my own family was not in the books. *Lord, You know better what is best for me; I will patiently wait for You to open the door. And if that means not being a husband, then give me the power to follow You in my celibacy with a content and obedient heart.*

• • •

The internship finished faster than I would've liked. Before I knew it, I was saying goodbye to the people who had welcomed me. During my last church service with them, my world collapsed. Mike gave me a filled-in report indicating my functioning during the internship. When asked what my strengths were, Mike said that I came across as highly personable and friendly, and that I am a good listener. He added that I have very good biblical insights, and that I know how to lead people further along their spiritual journey.

Mike's feedback affirmed me in ways that I had not expected. His words reached a dark place marred by years of self-loathing.

If someone as learned as Mike, someone with so much experience, sees those characteristics and abilities in me, then it must be true. I must be a good person after all. Like the healing words of a father, Mike's earnest statements made me realise that this is what I was looking for all along in my sexual partners, especially those old enough to be my dad. And so, I began praying for people like Mike to speak truth into my frame in a way that was life-giving and restorative.

• • •

For my last two weeks in Australia, Rory and I planned a holiday to Noosa, a ninety-minute drive north of Brisbane. We decided to rent a four-person campervan, equipped with a kitchenette and bathroom. Stopping every three hours for a fifteen-minute break, we reached Lake Macquarie caravan park by late afternoon. It felt like I was in heaven's waiting room; mesmerised by the beauty of the lake and the charm of the sunset reflected in the waves. In the morning, the sunbeams escaping from the horizon flooded our camper van with confounding golden light – the most beautiful moments in my life.

Spending this unforgettable minibreak with Rory showed us both how strong our relationship had become. However, I made Rory uncomfortable at times. I wanted him to express his emotions. He simply didn't know how to do that. I wanted him to know what was going on inside me after having given him cues. Rory would rather not talk about emotions at all. "It's too confronting for me, Alex. I freeze when you throw your plethora of emotions at me." Despite of these personality differences, we had found a way to make our relationship work.

"I'll find a way to interpret my feelings in ways that you can read them," I promised one morning before we headed off back to Canberra.

* * *

The most charming aspect of the whole experience in Australia was living with someone. I loved the mundane rituals of daily life with another man. I treasured eating dinner in the evening, under the decorative garden lights while the crickets chirped.

My last day in Canberra was one of the most emotionally troubled days of my life. The promise I made three months before had to be met; I had to end my romantic relationship with Rory. It felt daunting at first, but we helped each other go through the grieving process. A new future was about to be born.

The farewell at the airport felt rushed and superficial. Drying my tears before passing through security, I was overwhelmed with gratitude for my time in Australia, for Rory, for having discovered myself a bit more. It had changed my life and perspective. Confident, yet humble, I came back to Europe with a sense of freedom; my life unbridled by my volatile emotions.

* * *

I could hardly concentrate on finishing up my studies in Leuven – the only thing I could think of was finding ways of going back to Australia. A month after I returned, Rory told me that he'd love to get baptised, but that he'd wait until I could come back to Canberra. His impervious faith in my return gave me great hope. *Bring me back there, Father.*

While I was visiting my parents, Maya and I decided to catch up on what had happened in each other's lives. We booked a table at a restaurant in Crâng Park, in the centre of Buzău, an island on the lake that divided the park filled with flowers and people laughing.

I loved being able to see her. Stunning as ever, she chatted with confidence and passion. After we had caught up with the recent events, Maya asked warily: "Alex, why did our relationship never work?"

I knew she meant more than me not being sexually attracted to her. "I wish I had an answer, *May*. I love you more than you could ever imagine, but no matter how much I try to hone my emotions into being attracted to you, it doesn't work."

She looked at her hands resting on her bare legs. "But why though?"

"We both changed, *May*. After what Cezar did to me, you became like a sister to me. It felt almost like incest every time I tried to develop any romantic feelings for you. I've been thinking about it so often. Our imaginary kids are still somewhere at the back of my mind, playing uninterrupted. But I can't. I've hated myself for it for far too long already. I want to be released … also for your sake."

She listened attentively to every word I said, not lifting her head for one second. "Alright." I caught a shift in her gaze, like a switch. "Can I still continue to be your sister, though?" She looked at me, almost smiling, as if her facial muscles refused to follow a command.

"I'd love that. You will always retain your special place in my heart, *May* … always."

When we hugged, just before we said goodbye, it felt so final – as if it was the last time we'd see each other. I can still feel the peck she gave me on the left cheek, just as I was about to step onto the train. I wished life had been different – I was afraid I'd always be haunted by an ever-present *what if.*

• • •

The decision to study social work in Canberra felt natural. Before I knew it, I was enrolled in a master's course at Australian Catholic University in Canberra and back on an aeroplane to the place I felt I belonged. The connection I'd made to the land felt magical.

Canberra looked similar to Cislău – the mountains, the hilly areas, and the rivers. I felt like I'd been given a second chance. I was an invigorated person stepping towards a new horizon.

A HUNDREDFOLD

FOUR WEEKS AFTER I RETURNED to Australia, Rory and I decided to move to a hilly area in the south of Canberra. We wanted to have more space now that we'd moved in together. I craved decorating my home, going to furniture stores for ideas, and framing photographs I had taken during our holiday to the coast.

The idea of living together with someone I loved, albeit non-sexually, enveloped me in a sense of calmness and excitement. I named the new house *Luna*, because it was as beautiful as the moon. Close to a vast nature reserve, we had the most amazing view over the gorge. Being able to see the sunset from the kitchen, made me realise how blessed I was. I finally had what I'd always wanted: a place to call home, living with someone who accepted me for who I was and who loved me more than I deserved, a reconciled conscience, and a close relationship with God.

One spring morning, climbing up the hill on my way home, with one hand on the handlebar of the push bike and the other holding groceries, I wistfully looked around me. It felt as if I was back in Cislău, walking towards my favourite spots in the forest. Those fleeting sensations of being at home from my childhood, reanimated my thoughts again – the beautiful Wanniassa Hills bathing in the translucent spring sunlight, breathing out fresh air through eucalyptus leaves.

The next morning, as I was sipping from my flat white in a café with Rory, I was mentally transposed to a dream I had when I studied at the Bible school. In my dream I was conversing with this man I hadn't seen before. I remember speaking in English with him, focusing on the alien landscape outside. The wooden booth had the same features as the ones I was seeing now with Rory and the bar was identical. I began having a mild panic attack, realising that I had literally dreamt that moment years ago.

Noticing my distress, Rory looked puzzled when I explained what was going on inside me.

"I dreamt this scene years ago, Rory. It is surreal," I hyperventilated.

Rory looked puzzled, pushing his body back into the chair. "What do you mean?"

"I remember waking up, remembering all these details. It is either a very messed up déjà vu, or God must have a very weird sense of humour."

He frowned slightly, putting his hands back on the table. "I'm not sure what you want me to say."

"Nothing. It happened before at the Bible school, in Sibiu, but this was much more dramatic. It was so ... vivid. I need to go and get some air ... I'll be back in a second."

Just as I went outside to get more oxygen, I heard a faint voice inside my head saying: "It was meant to dispel any doubt you had, *son*. Your place is in Australia. Welcome home."

The panic dissipated instantaneously, leaving behind a trail of peace interweaved with a sense of pure joy. I didn't have to doubt anymore. From that moment on, I allowed my heart to feel at home in Canberra.

* * *

Two weeks after I moved into *Luna* with Rory, Mike decided to retire, leaving the church in a state of confusion and lacking leadership. Despite still feeling like an impostor, I loved that faith community. Because of the vacuum created by Mike's leaving, I decided to apply for the interim pastor position. Waiting for the reply of the pastoral search committee, I tried to gain insight from other members of the church regarding my compatibility for the job. Some were visibly enthusiastic, others were somewhat reticent.

During a discussion with a long-standing member of the church about the vacant position, the conversation turned to same-sex attracted ministers. Same as Mike, he also believed that a celibate Christian, attracted to their own sex, could not be a suitable candidate for their church. His words hit me like a wrecking ball.

In the weeks leading up to the decision of the pastoral search committee, it became apparent that I wouldn't feel comfortable being an interim pastor to a church that wouldn't accept me had they known about my sexuality. Despite feeling rejected when I read the email from the committee saying that my application was unsuccessful, I knew it was the right decision. I could no longer be part of a congregation that didn't recognise my pastoral abilities or would accept me as a celibate same-sex attracted Christian.

In the spur of the moment, thinking about moving church, I wrote a few verses which I called *Forgotten dreams*:

I wrote your name on an autumn leaf yesterday
As I let it fall in your frozen lake of neglect –
While my ears suffocated because of your memories'
affray
And your tacit words that will, one day, resurrect.

I slept with your naked thoughts last night
Under a canopy of days unspent together
While shooting stars set my sentiments alight.
I danced with your shadow's silhouette and your zephyr.

I embraced your glance one last time, as I awoke –
Knowing your presence will never again denude
My nights of their ethereal and diaphanous cloak.
Animated by my marine verisimilitude.

• • •

I met Harry, the pastor of another Baptist church in Canberra, during my internship. I was moved by his warmth in welcoming the other Baptist pastors at the fortnightly lunch event organised at his church. The pathos in his prayers inspired me to want to go and hear him preach. His sermons were theologically sound and incredibly personal. I knew I didn't have to look any further – it felt natural to move to his church. The congregation welcomed me with a wonderful cordiality.

The stained glass on each side of the building felt familiar – reconnecting with traces of memories from my childhood Orthodox church. The frankincense and the icons were missing, but the transcendental experience of being part of something bigger than myself was beating in sync with my own heart. The multicoloured reflections on the floor were a testament to the promise God had made me years ago on the bridge – the same God that promised Noah never to flood the earth anymore. The plan He had promised me was connected to the wonderful people I met in that quaint little church.

Weeks before I stepped into the church as a new member, I'd had a number of meetings with Harry. I was desperately looking for a mentor that would help me navigate this new episode of celibacy in my life. Prayerfully, I decided to talk to him about my sexuality.

Hesitantly, during our first mentorship session, I began telling him my life story. I could see the vivid sadness in his eyes, across from me, like a '70s wallpaper. When I finished, he almost let a tear go, and said: "Alex, you are the answer to our prayers!" He then told me that the church had been going through a process of biblically understanding sexual ethics, and that they had been praying for someone who was both Christian and same-sex attracted.

I felt incredibly affirmed by Harry's words. I'd prayed for a church where I wouldn't have to hide; embraced by a spiritual family that accepted me just as I was. Before I left his office, Harry's embrace marked the beginning of a new adventure.

• • •

Getting the role of the youth coordinator at the new church came like a silver lining. I loved serving my local faith community with the talents God had given me. The first day when I stepped into the youth room as a leader of the ministry, something inside me shifted. I felt I'd answered a call that had been beckoning me all my life. The tainted self-confidence and the ever-present self-loathing had been stopping me from embracing the person I was supposed to become. That day I *was* a new man. The expectant gaze on their faces was yet another echo of the promise "I've a big plan for your life."

Embracing the leadership position meant that I had to learn to accept the responsibility that came with it. The skills I'd acquired during the social work degree helped me understand the finer intricacies of leading people. After years of working on my own, I'd begun to study the art of negotiation – how much direction to give and what degree of autonomy my team should enjoy.

After a couple of months, I realised that I could bring my creativity to my vision for the youth ministry. I dreamed of a future when we would use photography, painting, drama, and acting to emulate our favourite stories of the Bible, in a fresh and personal manner.

● ● ●

Photography created and sustained me throughout my journey. Through the lens, I pictured a different world – a parallel reality in which I created beauty and harmony.

I wanted to honour my European home by calling my company New Holland Photography. Its name became a totem for my European roots living in the country named New Holland by the Dutch seafarer Abel Tasman in the seventeenth century. Through photography I got to know hundreds of people from diverse cultures, languages and religions.

The multitude of positive reviews affirmed me in ways I could have never anticipated. They helped me construct a healthy new self-confidence that propelled me onto a journey of self-improvement and self-acceptance.

● ● ●

From time to time, I still felt the need to be part of a camaraderie of brothers in Christ that struggled with understanding their sexuality, especially in relation to their faith. I'd looked online for local ministries that could put me in contact with such men. Most of my emails weren't returned.

But one afternoon, my phone rang showing the caller ID from someone living in Melbourne. At the other end, was a sweet-sounding forty-something year old lady who got my contact details from an organisation I'd previously contacted.

"You are definitely not alone, Alex. There are tens of thousands of men like you all over the world, seeking to reconcile their sexuality with their faith," she said.

"But how can I find them?" I asked, full of hope.

"I'll put you in contact with a pastor from Sydney and you can go from there."

I couldn't believe that one of my life's greatest dreams was about to be fulfilled. Her contact introduced me to multiple groups on Facebook. The lives of the men I grew to know through this connection have become an inspiration in my own journey. The bond that connected us in almost a mystical way, fostered the healing of parts of my heart that previously hurt, like a fire not properly put out.

Thanks to priceless friendships with these brothers, I began to appreciate and regard my sensitivity as being masculine, healthy and God-given. Gradually, I felt comfortable in the world of men, I was coming home to what I was designed to be.

Because my emotional reservoir was being filled by healthy

intimate male friendships, I was shocked to realise that I no longer craved the body of a man with the same intensity. I still desired to be embraced, seen, affirmed, but the sexual attraction felt like a magnet that had lost its power to attract.

• • •

On a beautiful Saturday summer morning, Rory and I went to the *Arboretum*, in the Molonglo Valley, to have lunch. Walking on the path that leads to the restaurant, Rory explained the history of the place, "Before Christmas 2001, this place was a dense pine forest. But the bushfires of 2001 and 2003 burned it to the ground. Now the area covers two hundred and fifty hectares designed to feature a hundred forests and a hundred gardens, focusing especially on rare species of trees and plants from all over the earth."

I looked at him, as if I had an *aha* moment. "So, it is a rebirth."

He smiled, looking at the big rusted sign *wide brown land* on top of the hill. "Yes, a bit like us."

"In what way?" I said.

"Well, we both came from dark and drought-stricken pasts. We are now reborn for a cause bigger than us. We are called to be the salt of the earth, harbouring hope and light for the people around us." A sense of contentment was tattooed on the corner of Rory's mouth.

"You do pay attention in church!" I joked.

"Yes, and to you. Even if most of the time I hide behind my Irish gravity."

I spotted a small building that looked like a postmodern iteration of Sydney Opera House. "What is that?"

Rory took a couple of seconds to respond. "I cannot

remember its name, but I know that it's mainly used for wedding ceremonies.

Once we approached it, I looked inside through the large glass doors. "If I ever get married, I want to do it here. Imagine being able to see the city from the *altar*."

Rory fell deep into thought. "What if you *never* get married, Alex? Will you still be happy? Will that make you feel like a man?"

I froze. Is he right, *Alex? Can you really be happy without a family and without having children?* Overlooking the city's panorama, out of nowhere, I had a vision. I was in front of a whiteboard, training other leaders in my church. I could read words like *happiness, home, accomplished, loved* written in red on the board. A feeling of appreciation and affection was etched on the people's faces. I was happy. I moved towards the window and saw the stars twinkling. I understood their coded message for me, *you are complete in Me, no one else can do that for you. Find your happiness in Me.*

The vision ended, my heart still singing. "Yes. I will be happy even if I don't get married and have my own children. I *know* I will."

Rory smiled and put his arm around me. "That's all I wanted to know. You've suffered enough, running for something you put all your hope in. Now, let's have something to eat before you come up with other deep subjects." He laughed and led the way to the restaurant.

* * *

I am in Brisbane, in one of the SpeedyCat ferries connecting St Lucia to Northshore Hamilton along the Brisbane River. Rory and I have decided to stay on the ferry for the entire one-and-a-half-hour journey.

"Would you mind if we look for a seat inside? You know I'm not comfortable so close to the balustrade," Rory says, heading for the door leading inside the ferry.

"No, not at all … as long as we find a window seat for me."

Rory scans the cabin, then points towards the far corner. "Look! There are two seats next to each other."

Fascinated by the view that rushes past me, I turn to Rory. "We should also have something like this in Canberra."

"I don't think we'll have a ferry in our *bush* capital any time soon."

Peace suddenly envelops me. I smile, letting a tear escape my eye.

"What happened? Are you alright?" Rory wipes it and looks at me concerned.

"No. I'm just *happy*. I don't have a single negative thought nagging at me. I feel so free, it frightens me. I got used to fighting those wretched voices, that now I wonder what to do with all this mental space and energy."

"I love seeing you like this, Alex. Never allow your past define you again." Rory puts his arm on my shoulder, gently squeezing it.

"Would you mind if I go on the deck for a while?"

"No. Don't lean too far forward!"

I move past him, squeezing him in the chair intentionally. "Yeah, yeah … dad!" We laugh.

Touching the cold silver balustrade, I see the city buzzing with people – like an invisible organism, every piece performing its function. I strangely feel part of it, as I inhale the salty breeze of the river. I feel alive.

Images from my childhood come to mind; hungry hyenas looking for prey. I realise they are powerless, my happiness unaffected by their hoot-laugh. I am no longer the little child – abused, beaten, sworn at, hated, unwanted. I am a man – utterly loved by the Man who sacrificed for me.

As the ferry leaves the Riverside terminal, I notice the Story Bridge. I am transported back to Cislău, to my own bridge. I notice a small child, crying and about to jump. All of a sudden, I see a Man appearing next to him. He whispers something in the child's ear, and then gives him a hug. They both cry. The Man disappears, as I make my way up.

He looks at me, wiping his tears away with the sleeve of his jumper. "He told me I am loved and that He has a plan for my life. Does He keep His promise?"

I smile, flooded with the loving memories collected along the years. "He does. He always will."

Little Alex disappears. The cold balustrade is now warm, as warm as my heart.

ABOUT THE AUTHOR

Alexandru Lupu was born in Romania. In 2018 he graduated from Evangelical Theological Faculty, Belgium. He moved to Australia where he studies Social Work at Australian Catholic University. Besides writing, Alexandru is a professional photographer, social worker, and youth leader. He now lives in Canberra, Australia.

Connect with Alexandru on:
www.alexandrulupu.com
@authoralexandrulupu

ACKNOWLEDGEMENTS

I would first like to acknowledge the Traditional Owners of the lands and waters on which I wrote this book. I acknowledge the Traditional Owners of country throughout Australia, and recognise their continuing connection to land, waters and culture. I pay my respects to their Elders past, present and emerging.

Thank you to my Heavenly Father whose love for me completely changed my existence. Thank you for that promise you made me more than a decade ago. You never failed to love me, comfort me, and accept me as a beloved child.

Thank you to Maya for you never tried to change me into someone I wasn't. I will always cherish the wonderful moments we shared together, especially those when you asked me to recite the poems I'd written.

Thank you to Gabriel Coțovan for having helped me to become the artist I am today. Thanks to you I started dreaming of one day writing a book.

Thank you to John and Matt for your unconditional love and for your support when I was an emotional volcano. Thanks to you, I learned how to love myself and embrace my past.

Thank you to Will, for believing in my writing before I believed in it myself. You awoke in me my love for the ocean, and for that I will be forever grateful.

Thank you to Jessica for making this book more readable to native English speakers. You really captured the essence of my ideas and made them even more beautiful.

Thank you to Alan for your friendship. You taught me that true intimacy is self-sacrificing. Thank you for opening your home to me and thank you for teaching me how to drive on the left side of the road.

And finally thank you to all the special people in my life who helped me become the man I am today.

Thanks for reading!

Please add a review of Amazon and let
me know what you thought!

• • •

Amazon reviews are extremely helpful for authors,
thank you for taking the time to support me and my work.
Don't forget to share your review on social media with
#sonofthecornfield
and encourage others to read my story too!

Lightning Source UK Ltd.
Milton Keynes UK
UKHW010630301120
374362UK00001B/111